MW00603510

UNSOLVED CRIMES

Publications International, Ltd.

Let's get social!

 @Publications_International

 @PublicationsInternational

 @BrainGames.TM

www.pilbooks.com

SOLVE THE UNSOLVABLE

Technology continues to play a key role in solving crimes. Criminal masterminds certainly use all manner of devices to perpetrate their crimes on unsuspecting subjects. Now it's your opportunity to play the role of lead investigator on a case!

You'll even have a chance to "go to the crime lab" to solve puzzles involving DNA sequences and fingerprints. Other puzzles in *Brain Games® Unsolved Crimes* allow you to assess your mastery of crime terminology, your deftness at wordplay, and your ability to juggle a multitude of hints and clues.

As you make your way through the book, some puzzle solutions will come to you faster than others. If you find yourself stuck, there's a handy answer key located at the back of the book. Are you ready to attempt solving the unsolvable? Grab a pencil, and commence sleuthing!

SUPER SLEUTHS

ACROSS

1. Fainthearted
7. Columbo and Uhura: abbr.
10. Cheer (for)
11. Land in the Thames
12. "Master Detective" of early radio and film
14. "___ mouse!"
15. Led Zeppelin's "Whole ___ Love"
16. Watch with open mouth
17. Michael Connelly's LAPD homicide detective
21. Revokes, in law
22. Hidden valleys
23. Dawn direction
27. Mickey Spillane's tough-guy gumshoe
29. Blood type letters
30. Black and orange bird
31. Letters on a returned check
32. In a spooky way

DOWN

1. "Rule, Britannia" writer
2. Pate de ___ gras
3. Scissors beater, in a game
4. Aleutian island
5. Five-ring-logo org.
6. "CSI" settings
7. Some coffee orders
8. Fancy shirt pin
9. Scottish valley
13. El ___ (cheap cigar, slangily)
16. Sneaker
17. "Dallas" star Larry
18. Bits of improv
19. Strongly smell like
20. "Get Shorty" actress Russo
23. It means "commander" in Arabic
24. Mine, in Marseilles
25. Hawk, as wares
26. Three in a deck
28. Milne's "Now We ___ Six"

A MURDERER IN THE HOUSE

Cryptograms are messages in substitution code. Break the code to read the message. For example, THE SMART CAT might become FVO QWGDF JGF if **F** is substituted for **T**, **V** for **H**, **O** for **E**, and so on.

TWCK F MVVI FB KWCK FM GRV WCB AGK KG WCHV C

JXUZVU COKXCIIL WCNNVRFRA FR GRV'B WGXBV, GRV

JFAWK CB TVII VRYGL FK, FM LGX SRGT TWCK F JVCR.

ANSWER ON PAGE 144.

BANK MAYHEM

A criminal mastermind who calls himself "Trixter" has hidden a stolen artifact in one of forty-five different safety deposit boxes at the local bank. Each box has a different number, and the miscreant has given the police a series of clues that will point to its hidden location. Using only these clues, find the one correct number—but be careful! Open the wrong box and the priceless artifact will be destroyed.

1. It is less than 90.

2. It is divisible by 2.

3. The first digit is greater than the second.

4. The square root of it is a whole number.

82	84	86	88	90	92	94	96	98
64	66	68	70	72	74	76	78	80
46	48	50	52	54	56	58	60	62
28	30	32	34	36	38	40	42	44
10	12	14	16	18	20	22	24	26

ANSWER ON PAGE 144.

THE GEM THIEF

A company that sold gems found that 6 types of gems had been stolen from their warehouse. There was 1 gem of the first type, 2 of the second type, 3 of the third type, 4 of the fourth type, 5 of the fifth type, and 6 of the sixth type. From the information given below, can you tell how many gemstones of each kind were taken?

1. There are three times as many pearls as sapphires.

2. There are three fewer agates than rubies.

3. There are even numbers of diamonds and turquoises.

4. There are more diamonds than turquoises.

ANSWER ON PAGE 144.

SNIFFING OUT THE EVIDENCE

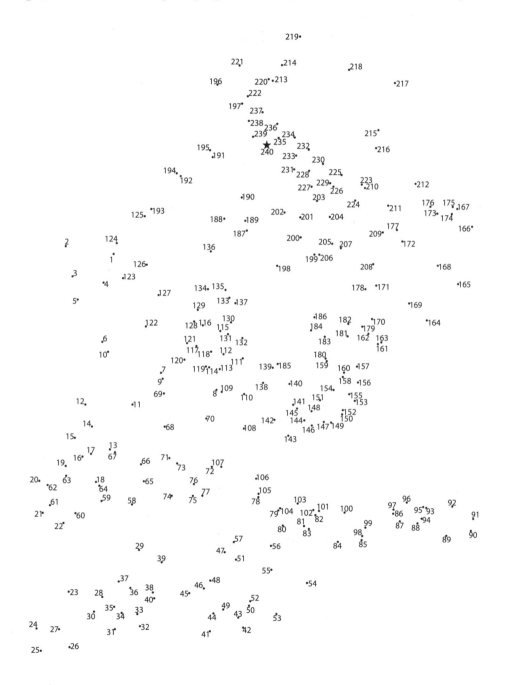

UNSOLVED IN AUSTRALIA

Every word listed is contained within the group of letters. Words can be found in a straight line horizontally, vertically, or diagonally. They may be read either forward or backward.

In 1898, three siblings, Michael, Norah, and Theresa "Ellen" Murphy, were killed shortly after Christmas near the town of Gatton, Queensland. They were returning home from a town dance that had been cancelled. Their brother-in-law went in search of them and found their bodies. Their horse had also been shot.

AUSTRALIA

BLUDGEONED

BOXING DAY

BRISBANE (Police)

DANCE

ELLEN

FARM

FIELD

GATTON

HANDKERCHIEFS
(The women's hands were tied.)

HARNESS STRAP

HORSE

MICHAEL

MURPHY

NORAH

QUEENSLAND

SHOT

STRANGLED

SULKY (Cart)

TELEGRAM

THEO FARMER (Laborer, suspect)

THOMAS DAY
(Alias for Theo Farmer)

WILLIAM M'NEILL
(Brother-in-law)

```
B E N A B S I R B L E H L W N D
E M R M I C H A E L A L P B N N
R B H O R S E C L R I S T L U A
G K L B W O N E N E R F R U Y L
A X J X C A N E N F W E Z D A S
T B A K D K S M T S M I I G D N
T N O I G S M E T R Z H Q E S E
O F B X S A L R A T X C N O A E
N V L T I E A F Z O E R O N M U
K S R L G N O L Y H Y E R E O Q
M A L R G E G K N S Q K A D H J
P I A L H F L D M B L D H M T L
W M E T I U Q W A Q B N M J H C
E D H E S B P Y F Y K A W O W K
A I L A R T S U A S Z H V H Z Z
J D F Y H P R U M R A F N Q P R
```

FINGERPRINT MATCH

Find the matching fingerprint(s). There may be more than one.

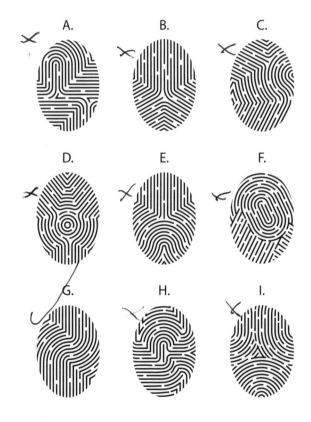

A.   B.   C.

D.   E.   F.

G.   H.   I.

ANSWER(S) ON PAGE 145.

WHAT CHANGED? (PART 1)

Study this picture for one minute, then turn the page.

WHAT CHANGED? (PART II)

(Do not read this until you have read the previous page!)

From memory, can you tell what changed between this and the previous page?

ANSWER ON PAGE 145.

DNA SEQUENCE

Examine the two images below carefully. Are these sequences a match or not?

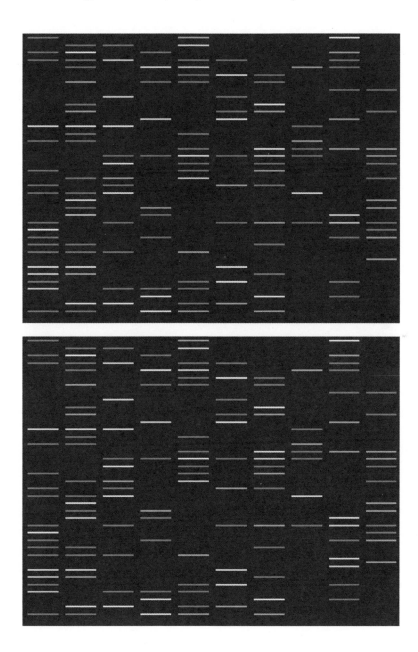

INTERCEPTION

You've intercepted a message between a criminal and his accomplice. But the message doesn't seem to make sense! Can you discover the meeting place hidden in the message?

CREEK

LIBRARY

BEACH

HOUSE

BANQUET

MANSION

ANNEX

DOWNS

STORE

CAFETERIA

ANSWER ON PAGE 145.

A HORRIFIC HOME INVASION (PART I)

Read this true crime account, then turn to the next page to test your knowledge.

About 45 miles north of Munich, Germany, a small Bavarian homestead named Hinterkaifeck became the site of a grisly and mysterious set of murders in 1922. Five members of the Gruber family from three generations were killed, along with their live-in maid Maria Baumgartner.

The killer may have been scoping out or living on the premises prior to the murder. A maid had quit six months before the murder when she heard sounds in the attic. A few days before the murder, father Andreas Gruber found tracks in the snow.

The new maid, Maria Baumgartner, arrived at the homestead on March 31, 1922, along with her sister who dropped her off. Maria's sister likely was the last person to see the Grubers alive—except, of course, the killer.

Sometime later on March 31, the killer lured most of the family members out to the barn one by one: Andreas Gruber, his wife Cazilia, their daughter Viktoria (a widow in her 30s), and Victoria's seven-year-old daughter, also named Cazilia. The killer also murdered Viktoria's two-year-old son Josef and Maria Baumgartner in the house itself, while they lay sleeping. Each was bludgeoned in the head by a mattock.

After a few days when the family members were absent from school and church, and after a repairman went to the household for an appointment without meeting anyone, one neighbor, Lorenz Schlittenbauer, sent his sons to the farm. When they didn't encounter anyone either, Lorenz went with two men, and they made the grisly discovery.

Based on the cattle being fed, evidence of lit fires in the hearth, and various stores being used, Munich police believed that the killer had stayed at the farm for several days after killing the inhabitants. Whoever it was, they had not robbed the house, as money was found left behind. Some forensic evidence had been compromised by locals who had moved the bodies and even made meals in the kitchen before the arrival of the police.

Some suspected strangers. Others suspected people closer to home. Lorenz Schlittenbauer was suspected because it was believed that he might have been the father of Viktoria's son. Some believed his actions when he discovered the bodies—and disturbed them—were suspicious and meant to make any investigation more difficult. The former maid suggested the Bichler brothers (one had helped at the potato harvest) and a friend of theirs might have done it; she was also suspicious of another set of brothers, the Thaler brothers, who were local burglars. Some even speculated that Viktoria's husband Karl Gabriel had not died during World War I as believed but had come back to commit the murders.

Whatever the case, the murders remain unsolved.

A HORRIFIC HOME INVASION (PART II)

(Do not read this until you have read the previous page!)

1. What was the name of the homestead?

   A. Hinterkaifeck

   B. Hunterkaifleck

   C. Hinterkaffleck

   D. Kinterhaifeck

2. Andreas Gruber's wife Cazilia was murdered in her bed.

   _____ True

   _____ False

3. The murder took place in this year.

   A. 1914

   B. 1918

   C. 1922

   D. 1926

4. The murder weapon was believed to be:

   A. A shovel

   B. A mattock

   C. An axe

   D. A knife

ANSWERS ON PAGE 145.

HOSTILITIES OF TELEVISION

Cryptograms are messages in substitution code. Break the code to read the message. For example, THE SMART CAT might become FVO QWGDF JGF if **F** is substituted for **T**, **V** for **H**, **O** for **E**, and so on.

LTTDRC B UGHPTH ER KTMTWDLDER XBR QTMF IEHO

EVV ERT'L BRKBCERDLUL. BRP DV ZEG QBWTR'K BRZ

BRKBCERDLUL, KQT XEUUTHXDBML IDMM CDWT ZEG LEUT.

ANSWER ON PAGE 146.

BADGE CARRYING

ACROSS

1. Friday or Bilko: abbr.
4. Kind of talk or rally
7. Otherwise
12. Atlantic City casino, with "The"
13. Clean air org.: abbr.
14. Tree stand
15. Mark the beginning of
17. Lint locale
18. Cop show with Angie Dickinson
20. Squashes a squeak
21. Historic realm of Europe: abbr.
22. Little shavers
24. Twists the arm of
28. Last of a drink
29. Federal oversight group: abbr.
30. Need to pay the piper
31. Haifa inhabitant
34. Knock-down-drag-out
36. JFK's predecessor: inits.
37. Like a Burns acquaintance
38. Cop show with Holly Hunter
42. Thigh-length skirts
43. Send through the skies
45. "_____ it goes"
46. Shine, in some ads
47. Sign of a hit: abbr.
48. City in the Ruhr valley
49. Baste, in a way
50. Brain test: abbr.

DOWN

1. "Fifth Beatle" Sutcliffe
2. Suck air
3. Cop show with Heather Locklear
4. Pauline's problems
5. Iliad and Odyssey
6. Window piece
7. Turn a deaf ear
8. Constitution writer
9. Temporary superstar
10. Roasting place
11. _____ Aviv
16. Peace Nobelist Wiesel
19. "Wait just a minute!"
22. Mai _____
23. NFL gains: abbr.
24. Cop show with Marg Helgenberger
25. Cop show with Kathryn Morris
26. Ram's partner
27. "Got it?"
29. Narrow valley
32. Counsel

33. He made light work
34. Journalist Edward R.
35. Jack of old oaters
37. Fleet-footed
38. Major no-nos

39. Interjects
40. Comics' bits
41. Emerald isle
42. Investors' Fannie
44. Kirk's journal

PERSON OF INTEREST

Spot the person of interest in the crowd scene.

ANSWER ON PAGE 146.

SEEN AT THE SCENE (PART I)

Study this picture for 1 minute, then turn the page.

handcuffs

drugs

bullet shells

SEEN AT THE SCENE (PART II)

(Do not read this until you have read the previous page!)

Which image exactly matches the picture from the previous page?

1.

2.

3.

4.

ANSWER ON PAGE 146.

A CRIME BOSS TOPPLES (PART 1)

Read this true crime account, then turn to the next page to test your knowledge.

Immigrating from Calabria, Italy, to Chicago as a teenager, Vincenzo Colosimo started as a petty criminal and eventually rose to power as the head of the mob organization that came to be known as the Chicago Outfit. In the States he went by Jim, and became known as Big Jim and Diamond Jim. Colosimo, who had an eye for jewelry and woman, was involved in prostitution and gambling. He married a madame, Victoria Moresco, and opened hundreds of brothels.

Colosimo ran the Chicago Outfit between 1902 and 1920. One of his trusted men was Johnny Torrio, Moresco's nephew, nicknamed "The Fox." Colosimo had pulled Torrio from New York in 1909 to counter a threat from the extortion racket Black Hand.

In 1920, Torrio disagreed with Colosimo about the future of the gang; Torrio saw opportunities in bootlegging, while Colosimo balked. Around that time, Colosimo and Moresco divorced and Colosimo remarried a singer.

In May 1920, Torrio alerted Colosimo about an arriving shipment at a restaurant Colosimo owned. However, Torrio was really setting him up for an ambush. Torrio and his protégé, Al Capone, arranged for Colosimo to be shot. The gunman was allegedly a man named Frankie Yale, but Capone himself may have committed the murder.

After Torrio arranged a showy funeral for the man whose murder he'd directed, he took over the Chicago Outfit. He only ran it for about five years when he was shot himself, and turned over control to Al Capone.

A CRIME BOSS TOPPLES (PART II)

(Do not read this until you have read the previous page!)

1. Colosimo ran his mob organization during these years.

   A. 1897–1905

   B. 1902–1909

   C. 1902–1920

   D. 1909–1920

2. Colosimo's first wife was named:

   A. Valentina Moresco

   B. Victoria Moresco

   C. Victoria Torrio

   D. Victoria Calabria

3. Torrio thought bootlegging during Prohibition was too risky and killed Colosimo before he could expand operations into that area.

   _____ True

   _____ False

4. Torrio lured Colosimo to this location to be murdered.

   A. Brothel

   B. Warehouse

   C. Lake

   D. Restaurant

ANSWERS ON PAGE 147.

TREASURE HUNT

The treasure hunter found six treasures in a row. At each find, he found a clue for the next treasure. Can you put the list of the six treasures he found in order, using the information below?

1. He did not search out the gold coins immediately after finding the rubies.

2. The clue buried with the silver necklace led him immediately to the bronze tiara.

3. He found the three stashes of gemstones (pearls, rubies, and sapphires) in the first three spots, but pearls were not first, rubies were not second, and sapphires were not third.

4. The gold coins were neither the first nor the last things he found.

ANSWER ON PAGE 147.

UNSOLVED IN 1876

Every word listed is contained within the group of letters. Words can be found in a straight line horizontally, vertically, or diagonally. They may be read either forward or backward.

British lawyer Charles Bravo was poisoned by antimony. He took several days to die, but gave no hint as to who might have poisoned him. His marriage with a wealthy wife was not a happy one, as he wanted more control of her money. One theory was that he was trying to poison her slowly (she had been unwell) and inadvertently poisoned himself.

**AGATHA CHRISTIE
(Mentions case)**

ANTIMONY

AUGUSTUS TURNER (Father)

BALHAM (Part of London)

BARRISTER

BRAVO

CHARLES

FLORENCE RICARDO (Wife)

**FROM HELL
(Comic book referencing case)**

HOUSEKEEPER

INQUEST

JOSEPH BRAVO (Stepfather)

LAUDANUM

MARY (Mother)

OPEN VERDICT

PAINFUL DEATH

POISONING

SCANDAL

TARTAR EMETIC

THE PRIORY (House)

UNSOLVED

WEALTHY

WILLFUL MURDER

WILLIAM GULL (Royal physician)

```
R W L A O V A R B H P E S O J R M
E K C P A I N F U L D E A T H O A
N Z F Q O H T I L J M B R A V O R
R R U L X P N H Y A Z A R Q E E Y
U D E D O Q E H E L U E H I N O M
T I M D U R T N A P P D T L L T T
S R W E R L E D V E R S A L A A G
U E S I A U N N E E I I E N R B G
T T R E L A M K C R R H O T U N Q
S S W Y C L E L H E M D A R I M U
U I S S N S I C U O R R I N Y N U
G R F E U O A A R F E I O C S E P
U R X O L H M F M M L S C O T U E
A A H Z T R L I E G I L L A K Y Q
C B K A V R A T T O U V I U R P T
I D G L V C I H P N E L P W A D N
K A V J X C O G C D A B L P X B O
```

FINGERPRINT MATCH

Find the matching fingerprint(s). There may be more than one.

ANSWER(S) ON PAGE 147.

INTERCEPTION

You've intercepted a message that is meant to reveal a location for an upcoming meeting between two criminal masterminds. The only problem is, the message shows many place names. Can you figure out the right location?

IVORY COAST

BUENOS AIRES

KUALA LUMPUR

SOLOMON ISLANDS

BURKINA FASO

NEW ORLEANS

CZECH REPUBLIC

NIZHNY NOVGOROD

MARSHALL ISLANDS

SOUTH AFRICA

ANSWER ON PAGE 147.

CRYPTO-LOGIC

Each of the numbers in the sequence below represents a letter. Use the mathematical clues to determine which number stands for which letter and reveal the encrypted word.

Hint: Remember that a / indicates divided by, and that all sums in parentheses must be done first.

83246457

$$M + H = N$$

$$R/2 = E$$

$$M \text{ squared} = I$$

$$O \times 2 = C$$

$$O + D = H$$

$$E \times M = R$$

$$E - 1 = C$$

$$N = 10$$

$$M \times 7 = R$$

ANSWER ON PAGE 147.

DNA SEQUENCE

Examine the two images below carefully. Are these sequences a match or not?

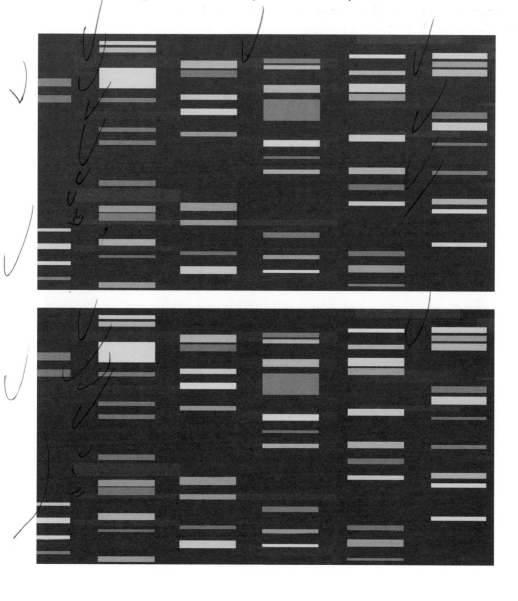

ANSWER ON PAGE 147.

MOST BOASTFUL

Cryptograms are messages in substitution code. Break the code to read the message. For example, THE SMART CAT might become FVO QWGDF JGF if **F** is substituted for **T**, **V** for **H**, **O** for **E**, and so on.

X UG KCPB C VZBCOXZI CUQXACRXGZ NGA CZSGZB

JKG KCV RKB XZRBTTXIBZHB RG MTCZ C LGE MAGM

BATS CZU RKB HGFACIB RG HCAAS XR GFR. CV TGZI CV

ZG GZB IBRV KFAR CZU RKB RCAIBR XV C ECZO GA CZ

XZVFACZHB HGQMCZS.

ANSWER ON PAGE 147.

WHAT CHANGED? (PART 1)

Study this picture for one minute, then turn the page.

WHAT CHANGED? (PART II)

(Do not read this until you have read the previous page!)

From memory, can you tell what changed between this and the previous page?

ANSWER ON PAGE 148.

JAIL CELL

Can you change just one letter on each line to transform the top word to the bottom word? Don't change the order of the letters, and make sure you have a common English word at each step.

JAIL

_____ what you pay to get out of jail

_____ a word often paired with base or foot

_____ this rings when class is done

CELL

BAIL BOND

Change just one letter on each line to go from the top word to the bottom word. Do not change the order of the letters. You must have a common English word at each step.

BAIL

_____

_____

_____

BOND

If you can't do it four steps, can you do it in five?

ANSWERS ON PAGE 148.

WOMEN OF MYSTERY

ACROSS

1. Watch pocket
4. Likely
7. _____ point (center of activity)
12. Eisenhower's nickname
13. Caviar, e.g.
14. Black
15. Writer Sue of the Kinsey Millhone alphabet mysteries
17. Greene of "Bonanza"
18. H.H. Munro's nom de plume
19. Arrive at the curb
21. In that place
23. Thwack a fly
26. Dell alternative
29. Genesis garden
30. Actress Garr
31. Actor Hawke
33. Singer K.T. _____
34. Ripped
35. Razor choice
38. Set down
39. Heroic tale
40. Egyptian capital
42. "Button your lip!"
44. Page

48. Preminger and Kruger
50. Writer Ruth whose "A Dark-Adapted Eye" won the '87 Edgar
52. Gullible
53. "Born in the _____"
54. Herbert Hoover's First Lady
55. Complies
56. Farm enclosure
57. Perceive

DOWN

1. Newton fruits
2. Gumbo veggie
3. Bird's bill
4. MoMA display
5. All tuckered out
6. Secure faculty status
7. Plummeted
8. Certain woodwind musicians
9. Crime novelist Patricia who writes the Dr. Kay Scarpetta series
10. Legendary advice columnist Landers
11. Soap ingredient
16. Temper tantrum
20. Ex-QB Dawson
22. Fowl female
24. Diva's song

25. Itsy-bitsy

26. Dole (out)

27. On the crest of

28. Author Agatha who created Hercule Poirot and Jane Marple

32. Pizza tidbit

33. Galley propeller

35. Behave

36. Zodiac sign in May

37. Most fully matured

41. On its last legs

43. Brings into play

45. Squirmy catches

46. Burn soother

47. Ventilation duct

48. "Double Fantasy" singer

49. Diet cola introduced in 1963

51. Negative vote

1	2	3		4	5	6		7	8	9	10	11
12				13				14				
15			16					17				
18					19		20					
			21	22					23		24	25
26	27	28		29					30			
31			32					33				
34					35	36	37			38		
39					40			41				
		42		43					44	45	46	47
48	49					50		51				
52						53				54		
55						56				57		

ANSWERS ON PAGE 148.

PERSON OF INTEREST

Spot the person of interest in the crowd scene.

ANSWER ON PAGE 149.

MURDER AT LAVA LAKE (PART 1)

Read this true crime account, then turn to the next page to test your knowledge.

In the winter of 1923 and 1924, three fur trappers were sharing a log cabin in the wilds of Deschutes National Forest in Oregon: Edward Nickols (age 50), Roy Wilson (35) and Dewey Morris (25). Nickols was seen selling furs in the town of Bend, where the men lived, the week before Christmas. A man traveling by snowshoe, Allen Wilcoxen, stopped by the log cabin in mid-January, and said he had met the men and they were all in good spirits. He was the last person known to see them alive.

In April 1924, none of the men had been seen for some time. Dewey Morris's brother Innis was concerned that he hadn't heard from Dewey. Others noted that some mink traps in the area had been left untouched for some time. When a search team went to the cabin, they didn't find any of the men there. Frozen remains of animals had been left behind in traps; food had been left in pots on the stove; and a sled and some equipment were missing. Most alarming of all, a claw hammer with blood on it had been left behind in an empty fox pen.

Deschutes County Sheriff Clarence Adams joined the search, which expanded to the shore of Lava Lake where the missing sled was found. It was obvious that a hole had been chopped in the ice on the surface of the lake. When the search party set out in boats on the thawing lake, they found the bodies of the men floating in their watery graves.

It was believed that the men died in late December or early January. The deaths were brutal: all the men had been shot, but also suffered blunt force trauma, presuambly from the hammer. Near the lake, searchers found blood, hair, and a tooth. Some suspected two killers had been involved, one using a shotgun, the other a pistol.

Police first suspected a woodsman who camped nearby, but he had an alibi. Attention then focused on a trapper who had quarreled with Nickols previously, Lee Collins. It transpired that "Lee Collins" was an alias for a man named Charles Kimzey, who had been in trouble with the law before. In fact, he'd escaped from a prison in Idaho. Kimzey was also wanted for a robbery where he hired a stagecoach driver for transport, then almost killed him and left him for dead, stealing the car. A man matching Kimzey's description had been seen in Portland in January 1924 selling fox furs believed to be stolen from Nickols, Morris, and Wilson. However, Kimzey had dropped off the map, and could not be found for questioning.

He was spotted almost a decade later in 1933 in Montana, and sent to Oregon. By that time, the fur deal in Portland could not identify him positively. Though Kimzey was sent to prison for his assault on the driver, he was never charged with the murders of Nickols, Wilson, and Morris. The trail had gone cold.

MURDER AT LAVA LAKE (PART II)

(Do not read this until you have read the previous page!)

1. The log cabin was found in this National Forest.

_____

2. Nickols sold furs in this town shortly before Christmas.

_____

3. Besides Nickols, what were the names of the two other men who were killed?

_____

_____

4. Charles Kimzey was going by this alias.

_____

ANSWERS ON PAGE 149.

FINGERPRINT MATCH

Find the matching fingerprint(s). There may be more than one.

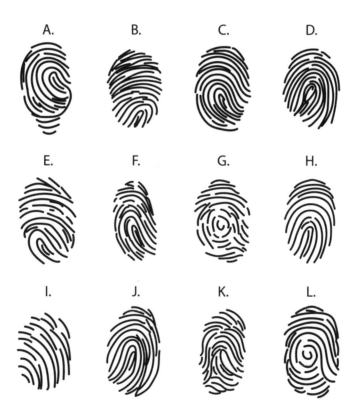

A.

B.

C.

D.

E.

F.

G.

H.

I.

J.

K.

L.

ANSWER(S) ON PAGE 149.

UNSOLVED IN 1841

Every word listed is contained within the group of letters. Words can be found in a straight line horizontally, vertically, or diagonally. They may be read either forward or backward.

Edgar Allan Poe's detective story "The Mystery of Marie Rogêt" was based on a real-life murder of a woman in her early 20s named Mary Rogers, whose body was found in the Hudson River. Some people theorized gang violence; others that her body was dumped when an abortion went wrong. Her fiancé later committed suicide.

BEAUTIFUL

BOARDING HOUSE

CLERK

CUSTOMERS

DANIEL PAYNE (Fiancé)

DISAPPEARED

DUPIN (Poe's sleuth)

GANG VIOLENCE

HUDSON RIVER

JAMES FENIMORE COOPER
(Customer)

LAUDANUM (Overdose)

MARY

NEW YORK

PUBLICIZED

ROGERS

SENSATIONAL

TOBACCO STORE (Workplace)

WASHINGTON IRVING
(Customer)

```
R N C U S T O M E R S M Z V Y W W N E
D E O M D K K O Q I W O B D D T V N R
P W P Q T I R I N E W Y O R K L H I O
U N D O W I H E S M U V R S W U F P T
S R R W O N U U L W V S Z P K F K U S
E U O W K C V G D C T K L X X I N D O
N S B G E F E E A S J T D V X T I R C
S Y W D E R C R P N O X B K X U I H C
A G N I V R I N O T G N I H S A W O A
T Y R A M G S Q K M A V R X R E N R B
I V U Y O T A I J J I V I I L B D I O
O O M U N A D U A L X N E O V E A H T
N D E Z I C I L B U P V E M L E A H Z
A L D E R A E P P A S I D F E E R B R
L X H Q K Y R L G T F T A W S W N M P
C W B B O A R D I N G H O U S E I C I
Y J E F P D H O I U J B E F S X M K E
E I N D T I Z W L K L S Y T Q M X A R
O J H D A N I E L P A Y N E O J P X J
```

MOTEL HIDEOUT

A thief hides out in one of the 45 motel rooms listed in the chart below. The motel's in-house detective received a sheet of four clues, signed "The Logical Thief." Using these clues, the detective found the room number—but by that time, the thief had fled. Can you find the thief's motel room more quickly?

1. The number is odd, but one digit is even.

2. The number is not a multiple of 3.

3. The number is not prime.

4. The sum of the digits is less than 10.

51	52	53	54	55	56	57	58	59
41	42	43	44	45	46	47	48	49
31	32	33	34	35	36	37	38	39
21	22	23	24	25	26	27	28	29
11	12	13	14	15	16	17	18	19

ANSWER ON PAGE 149.

INTERCEPTION

You've intercepted a message that is meant to reveal a location for an upcoming meeting between two criminal masterminds. The only problem is, the message shows many place names. Can you figure out the right location?

ERITREA

ITALY

FRANCE

FUNAFUTI

ESTONIA

LATVIA

TONGA

OMAN

WASHINGTON, DC

EGYPT

REYKJAVIK

ANSWER ON PAGE 149.

CRYPTO-LOGIC

Each of the numbers in the sequence below represents a letter. Use the mathematical clues to determine which number stands for which letter and reveal the encrypted word.

Hint: Remember that a / indicates divided by, and that all sums in parentheses must be done first.

72159

M + U = T

S - D = R

T squared = D + S

U/1 = 1

G - U = T

3M = S

R X U = 2

R + U = M

ANSWER ON PAGE 149.

DNA SEQUENCE

Examine the two images below carefully. Are these sequences a match or not?

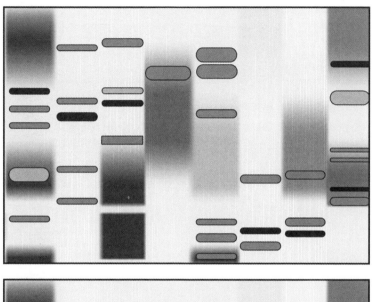

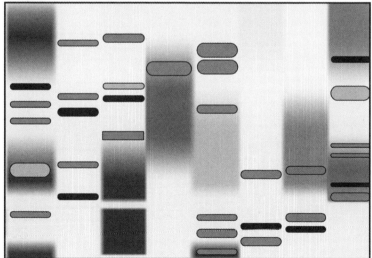

ANSWER ON PAGE 150.

THE GEM THIEF

A company that sold gems found that 5 types of gems had been stolen from their warehouse. There was 1 gem of the first type, 2 of the second type, 3 of the third type, 4 of the fourth type, and 5 of the fifth type. From the information given below, can you tell how many gemstones of each kind were taken?

1. There are not 3 emeralds.

2. There are more than 3 diamonds.

3. There are two more pieces of topaz than there are turquoises.

4. There is one more ruby than there are pieces of topaz.

ANSWER ON PAGE 150.

SEEN AT THE SCENE (PART I)

Study this picture for 1 minute, then turn the page.

SEEN AT THE SCENE (PART II)

(Do not read this until you have read the previous page!)

Which image exactly matches the picture from the previous page?

1.

2.

3.

4.

ANSWER ON PAGE 150.

TRACK THE FUGITIVE

The investigator is tracking the fugitive's past trips in order to find and recover information that was left behind in five cities. Each city was visited only once. Can you put together the travel timeline, using the information below?

1. The two cities in Texas were not visited consecutively.

2. Memphis was visited sometime before Baltimore.

3. Fresno and San Antonio were visited in that order, but not back-to-back.

4. El Paso was visited sometime after Memphis.

5. El Paso was visited sometime before Fresno.

ANSWER ON PAGE 150.

SOMETHING IS AFOOT

ACROSS

1. Weeknight comic that replaced Carson
5. Do laps, perhaps
9. "For _____ a jolly good fellow"
12. One-named singer
13. Party day and night
15. Save for a rainy day
17. _____ the line (obeyed)
18. Come after
19. Garden sticker
22. Rower's tools
24. With 34-Across, do a chore on board
26. Mas' opposite numbers
29. Out for the night
30. 2006 Winter Olympics site
33. "Who am _____ say?"
34. See 24-Across
36. El _____, Texas
38. Boise's state
39. Ed of "Up"
42. Defeat decisively
44. Stickup men may wear them
49. Nonmember
50. Mop's companion
51. Govt. construction group
52. Quick message
53. Water whirled

DOWN

1. French article
2. Rocker Brian
3. Big Apple letters
4. Durable wood source
5. Kind of gin
6. Computer screen section
7. "_____ got it!"
8. Teri Hatcher's Susan on "Desperate Housewives"
9. Hem's partners
10. Jacob's twin
11. Eye problem
14. Screechers in the bleachers
16. French newspaper, with "Le"
19. Asian cuisine
20. Emcee
21. Norse port
23. Initial stake
25. Decides to leave, with "out"
26. Type size
27. Egyptian cross
28. "Could be better"

31. Disgust

32. Bureaucratic tangle

35. Stinging insect

36. Iron pumpers develop them

37. Alan of "Little Miss Sunshine"

39. Starting from the date

40. Macho man

41. "_____ creature was stirring…"

43. Shrek, for instance

45. Wedding words

46. Bummed out

47. Tease playfully

48. Devious

PERSON OF INTEREST

Spot the person of interest in the crowd scene.

ANSWER ON PAGE 150.

PRIEST, GANGSTER, POLITICIAN (PART 1)

Read this true crime account, then turn to the next page to test your knowledge.

Anthony D'Andrea (born Antonio in Sicily in 1872) lived a fascinating life. After studying law in Siciliy, he immigrated to the United States, where he attended seminary before becoming ordained in 1899 in Chicago. However, when he met a young woman named Lena and fell in love, he quickly left the priesthood and became a language teacher and translator who helped assist his fellow Italian American immigrants with legal issues.

D'Andrea became involved in organized crime at some point. In 1902, he was arrested as the head of a counterfeiting gang and sent to prison. When he was released a year later, he continued his life of crime. D'Andrea held various positions of power, both legal and illegal; he was the local president of a union, but also a Mafia boss. He first ran for alderman of Chicago's nineteenth ward in 1916, dropping out when the press covered his ties to organized crime. When he ran for alderman again, his opponent was a popular saloon keeper named John Powers. The struggle between the two men turned bloody and violent. Between 1916 and 1921, more than thirty casualties were reported in the so-called "Aldermen's Wars."

In 1921, D'Andrea announced his retirement from politics. However, in May, he was shot and killed by an unknown assailant.

PRIEST, GANGSTER, POLITICIAN (PART II)

(Do not read this until you have read the previous page!)

1. D'Andrea was born in this year.

_____

2. D'Andrea was arrested for this crime in 1902.

_____

3. D'Andrea tried to achieve political power by becoming an alderman in this ward.

_____

4. D'Andrea's opponent was named:

_____

ANSWERS ON PAGE 151.

AN UNSOLVED CRASH

Cryptograms are messages in substitution code. Break the code to read the message. For example, THE SMART CAT might become FVO QWGDF JGF if F is substituted for **T**, **V** for **H**, **O** for **E**, and so on.

OC 1923, M VDRCH, PMJOCH MSOMLDJ POQP ML LNQ MHQ DG 31.

W.N. PQEMV DTCQP MC MOJGOQEP, FQJGDJAQP WMJCKLDJAOCH

KLRCLK, MCP POP KLRCL MSOMLODC OC LNQ ADSOQK. NQ MEKD

LJMOCQP DLNQJ FOEDLK OC KLRCL MSOMLODC GDJ NDEEVTDDP.

OC 1923, NQ TMK PDOCH M KNDT TNQC NOK FEMCQ FERAAQLQP

LD LNQ HJDRCP OC LNQ AOPPEQ DG M EDDF-PQ-EDDF, BOEEOCH

NOA MCP NOK FMKKQCHQJ. OL TMK KDDC GDRCP LD WQ CD

KOAFEQ ZJMKN. FOCK OC LNQ FEMCQ'K TOCHK TQJQ GDRCP LD

WQ DG KRWKLMCPMJP KOXQ, FDOCLOCH LD KMWDLMHQ. CD

DCQ TMK QSQJ ZNMJHQP TOLN LNQ ZJOAQ.

ANSWER ON PAGE 151.

UNSOLVED IN 1682

Every word listed is contained within the group of letters. Words can be found in a straight line horizontally, vertically, or diagonally. They may be read either forward or backward.

Alessandro Stradella was an Italian composer who was stabbed to death at the Piazza Banchi by an unknown killer hired by a noble family, the Lomellinis. He had been previously attacked by assassins in 1677 after he had an affair with the mistress of a powerful nobleman.

AFFAIRS

AGNESE VAN UFFELE (Mistress)

ALESSANDRO

ASSASSINS

BAROQUE

CANTATAS

COMIC OPERA

COMPOSER

CONCERTO GROSSO

CONTARINI (Nobleman)

FLEE ROME

GENOA

HIRED KILLER

LOMELLINI

OPERA

ORATORIO

PIAZZA BANCHI

ROME

SERENATA

SONATA DE CHIESA

STABBING

STRADELLA

TURIN

TUSCAN

VENICE

```
E M O R E E L F F T E M O R A A
S Z G S N I S S A S S A H G S H
A L E S S A N D R O V I N E C E
R C B E T U R I N G R E I A O V
L O A C G C H Z N E S H L O N S
O M R I E Y L I D E C L A R C A
M I O N N A B K V E E R C A E T
E C Q E O B I A D D E Q R T R A
L O U V A L N A A P B T O O T T
L P E T L U T R O C O D A R O N
I E S E F A T N A C S U T I G A
N R R F N S A F F A I R S O R C
I A E O B R E S O P M O C U O D
Y L S H C O N T A R I N I J S U
E L I H C N A B A Z Z A I P S T
S E R E N A T A Y Q E C N A O F
```

FINGERPRINT MATCH

Find the matching fingerprint(s). There may be more than one.

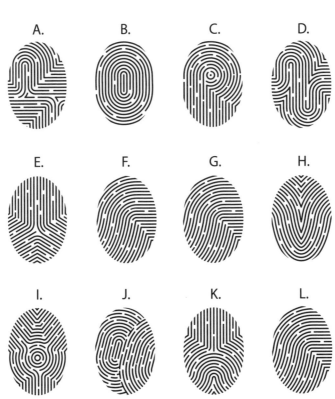

A.   B.   C.   D.

E.   F.   G.   H.

I.   J.   K.   L.

ANSWER(S) ON PAGE 151.

OVERHEARD INFORMATION (PART I)

Read the story below, then turn the page and answer the questions.

The detective overheard the thief tell his accomplice about the different places where he stashed the loot. He said, "The Piaget wristwatch and Meissen figurines are in the safe in the condo on Lakewood Drive. The pearls are inside a carefully resealed oyster tin in the pantry in the summer house out on Miller Drive. The diamonds are in the toolbox in the garage of the house on Wentworth Avenue, and the first edition map is in the sewing room there, behind the hutch."

OVERHEARD INFORMATION (PART II)

(Do not read this until you have read the previous page!)

1. What two items are found in the condo?

       A. Piaget wristwatch and Meissen figures

       B. Piaget figures and Meissen wristwatch

       C. Pearls and map

       D. Diamond and map

2. The pearls are inside this type of tin.

       A. Tuna

       B. Oyster

       C. Clam

       D. Sardines

3. The diamonds are found at a place on this street.

       A. Lakewood Drive

       B. Lakewood Avenue

       C. Miller Avenue

       D. Wentworth Avenue

4. The map is found in this location.

       A. A toolbox

       B. A spare bedroom

       C. A safe

       D. Behind a hutch

ANSWERS ON PAGE 151.

MOTEL HIDEOUT

A thief hides out in one of the 45 motel rooms listed in the chart below. The motel's in-house detective received a sheet of four clues, signed "The Logical Thief." Using these clues, the detective found the room number—but by that time, the thief had fled. Can you find the thief's motel room more quickly?

1. The number is either a multiple of 3 or one of the digits is 3, but not both.

2. Either both digits are odd or both digits are even.

3. When you multiply the digits together, the result is an even number.

4. The first digit is larger than the second.

51	52	53	54	55	56	57	58	59
41	42	43	44	45	46	47	48	49
31	32	33	34	35	36	37	38	39
21	22	23	24	25	26	27	28	29
11	12	13	14	15	16	17	18	19

INTERCEPTION

You've intercepted a message that is meant to reveal a location for an upcoming meeting between two criminal masterminds. The only problem is, the message shows many place names. Can you figure out the right location?

MANILA

INCHEON

STUTTGART

ROME

EGYPT

ANSWER ON PAGE 152.

WHAT CHANGED? (PART I)

Study this picture for one minute, then turn the page.

WHAT CHANGED? (PART II)

(Do not read this until you have read the previous page!)

From memory, can you tell what changed between this and the previous page?

ANSWER ON PAGE 152.

PICK YOUR POISON

There are five bottles before you, but they've gotten jumbled up. Poison is found in one of them. If you arrange them from left to right, following the instructions given below, you will be able to know where the poison is found.

1. The blue bottle is separated from the purple bottle by exactly one other bottle.

2. The green bottle in the middle does not contain the poison.

3. The yellow bottle is somewhere to the left of the green bottle.

4. The red bottle, which neither contains the poison nor is next to the bottle with the poison, is to the immediate right of the blue bottle.

5. The poison is in the second bottle from the left.

CRYPTO-LOGIC

Each of the numbers in the sequence below represents a letter. Use the mathematical clues to determine which number stands for which letter and reveal the encrypted word.

Hint: Remember that a / indicates divided by, and that all sums in parentheses must be done first.

564184

4 is a consonant

6 is a vowel

2R = E

4M = 20

4D = R

E - 2 = U

D + 4 = M

ANSWER ON PAGE 152.

FIND THE WITNESS

On Dyson Drive, there are 5 houses that are identical to each other. You need to follow up with a witness, Tom Wright, but without any address on the doors you are not sure which house to approach. You know that from a previous statement that Wright lives with his husband and has one child. The staff at the corner ice cream shop and your own observations give you some clues. From the information given, can you find the right house?

A. No children live in either corner house.

B. A retired couple live in the middle house, and the wife likes to bake goodies for the street.

C. The retired couple lives 2 houses to the right of the semi-famous singer.

D. When the school was doing a fundraiser, the semi-famous singer bought cases of chocolate bars both from their next-door neighbors and from the Wrights.

| House A | House B | House C | House D | House E |

ANSWER ON PAGE 152.

UNSOLVED IN 1678

Every word listed is contained within the group of letters. Words can be found in a straight line horizontally, vertically, or diagonally. They may be read either forward or backward.

Sir Edmund Berry Godfrey, an English magistrate, was found in a ditch, strangled and then impaled with his own sword after death. He had not been robbed. It was a time of religious strife, and three Catholics were executed for the crime, although later historians believed them innocent. Other theories involved a revenge plot by an Earl Godfrey had prosecuted and that Godfrey had committed suicide and it had been covered up by his family.

BERRY

BRUISES

DITCH

EDMUND

ELIZABETH (Maid)

GODFREY

HENRY (Secretary)

IMPALEMENT

KENT (Birthplace)

KNIGHTHOOD

MAGISTRATE

MURDER

PERJURY

POPISH PLOT

PRIMROSE HILL (Site of death)

REVENGE

SAMUEL PEPYS (Pepys's famous diary mentions Godfrey.)

SUICIDE

SWORD

TITUS OATES

```
E Y R U J R E P U L O X G G L E
Y T P Y S A M U E L P E P Y S M
E E R O R G M S U P H R J T J C
A F T U P N O O W X Q P D I Y J
P Z V A C I E D Z O R R J T R N
E K N E R A S H F I R D R U R X
H D B D Z T X H M R O D E S E S
C D U M G F S R P O E F V O B E
T C K U D X O I H L X Y E A H S
I H T N B S P T G E O S N T D I
D Q I D E A H E N A D T G E U U
E R W H C G O H T E M I E S O R
D L I Y I Z T X D G K P C Z X B
S L T N M X M U R D E R W I J R
L E K V E L I Z A B E T H Z U A
W T N E M E L A P M I V V W Q S
```

DNA SEQUENCE

Examine the two images below carefully. Are these sequences a match or not?

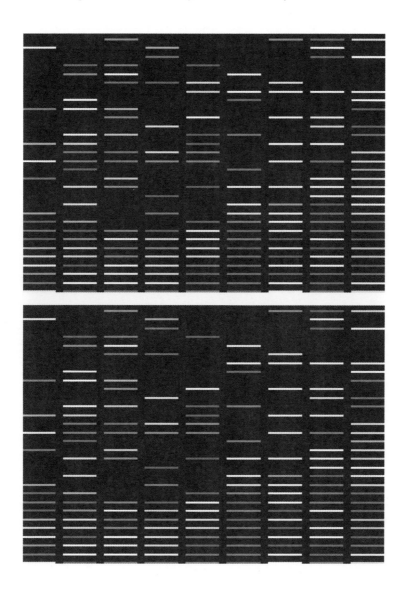

ANSWER ON PAGE 152.

SEEN AT THE SCENE (PART 1)

Study this picture for 1 minute, then turn the page.

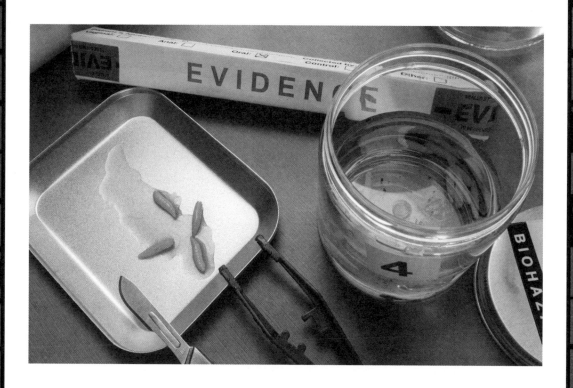

SEEN AT THE SCENE (PART II)

(Do not read this until you have read the previous page!)

Which image exactly matches the picture from the previous page?

1.

2.

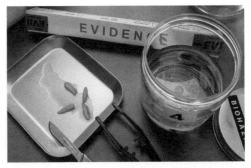

3.

4.

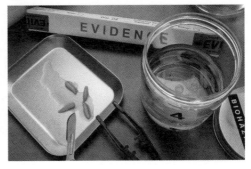

ANSWER ON PAGE 153.

THE GREEN BICYCLE CASE (PART I)

Read this true crime account, then turn to the next page to test your knowledge.

On July 5, 1919, a 21-year-old woman named Bella Wright was shot and killed near the village of Little Stretton, Leicestershire, England. She worked in a nearby rubber factory. Because she worked the late shift, she sometimes spent her afternoons cycling around the villages nearby to visit friends and relatives.

On the evening of July 5, a farmer named Joseph Cowell discovered Wright's body next to her bicycle. At first, Cowell thought she had fallen off her bike or that a motorist had run her off the road. He alerted the police and a doctor. While the doctor—investigating by candlelight—thought that Wright had simply been involved in an accident, the police constable, Alfred Hall, was less sure. Returning to the area in the daylight hours, he diligently searched for signs of potential foul play—and he found a bullet embedded in the ground. In the daytime, when blood had been washed off Wright's face, it became clear that she had been shot beneath the eye.

Once relatives identified Wright as the victim, police began to retrace her steps on the day of the murder. On that day, Wright had been bicycling to the village of Gaulby to visit her uncle, George Measures. Her uncle reported that when she came to visit, she had been accompanied by a stranger, a man she had met en route, who waited for her outside the cottage. The two left around 8:50 PM; Wright's body was found about a half-hour later. The uncle would later say that he had not liked the looks of the young man, and that Wright had reported him an innocuous companion but added that she might try to "give him the slip." Other witnesses also reported seeing Wright on the road in the company of a man on a green bicycle.

Based on witness descriptions, police asked the press to distribute a description of a man in his late 30s, wearing a gray suit and black boots. They also began searching bicycle shops to try to track down the owner of the green cycle. On July 10th, they had one hit, when bicycle repairman Harry Cox informed police that he'd repaired a similar bicycle.

In February 1920, the tow-rope of a barge in a canal snagged on the frame of a bicycle. When the canal was dragged, other bicycle parts were discovered. Though the serial number had been filed off, from traces police were able to track down the owner of the green bicycle: a man named Ronald Light.

Though Light originally denied both owning a green bicycle and having been in the area on that date, much less meeting Wright, overwhelming evidence and eyewitness testimony said differently. Police found he had sold or destroyed all the clothing he used on that day. His Army holster and bullets that matched the bullet found at the scene were also found in the canal where he had tried to destroy his bike.

At trial, Light changed his story, saying he had met Wright and helped her with her bike. He attested that they had parted ways after leaving her uncle's, and that his lies and destruction of evidence simply resulted panic when he read about Wright's murder in the newspaper. His defense attorney argued that there was no motive for the crime, and suggested that an unknown shooter might have fired the fatal shot, that the bullet that killed Wright could have been from a rifle from afar rather than Light's service revolver. Light was acquitted.

THE GREEN BICYCLE CASE (PART II)

(Do not read this until you have read the previous page!)

1. Bella Wright worked at this job.

>   A. Maid
>
>   B. Factory worker
>
>   C. Shopgirl
>
>   D. Lady's companion

2. What was the name of the farmer who found Wright's body?

>   A. Alfred Hall
>
>   B. Joseph Cowell
>
>   C. George Measures
>
>   D. Henry Cox

3. What was the name of Wright's uncle?

>   A. Alfred Hall
>
>   B. Joseph Cowell
>
>   C. George Measures
>
>   D. Henry Cox

4. The bike was found in this month and year.

>   A. July 1919
>
>   B. September 1919
>
>   C. February 1920
>
>   D. June 1920

ANSWERS ON PAGE 153.

UNSOLVED IN NEW JERSEY

Cryptograms are messages in substitution code. Break the code to read the message. For example, THE SMART CAT might become FVO QWGDF JGF if **F** is substituted for **T**, **V** for **H**, **O** for **E**, and so on.

JE 1922, NKR YFTJRM FP Z AZE ZET Z SFAZE SRIR PFOET JE Z PJRBT.

NKRV KZT YFNK YRRE MKFN. Z KZN XFQRIRT NKR AZE'M PZXR,

ZET KJM XZBBJEL XZIT SZM PFOET ZN KJM PRRN. NKR AZE, RTSZIT

KZBB, SZM ZE RGJMXFGZBJZE GIJRMN AZIIJRT NF PIZEXRM KZBB.

NKR SFAZE, RBRZEFI AJBBM, AZIIJRT NF DZARM AJBBM, SZM Z

ARAYRI FP NKR XKOIXK XKFJI. NKR NSF KZT YRRE KZQJEL ZE

ZPPZJI, ZET NKRJI BFQR BRNNRIM SRIR BRPN YRNSRRE NKRJI

YFTJRM. SKJBR PIZEXRM ZET KRI YIFNKRIM SRIR ZXXOMRT ZET

NIJRT PFI NKR XIJAR JE 1926, NKRV SRIR ZXHOJNNRT PFI BZXC

FP RQJTREXR ZET YRXZOMR SJNERMMRM XBZJART NKZN FER

YIFNKRI KZT YRRE PJMKJEL SJNK NKRA.

THE GEM THIEF

A company that sold gems found that 5 types of gems had been stolen from their warehouse. There was 1 gem of the first type, 2 of the second type, 3 of the third type, 4 of the fourth type, and 5 of the fifth type. From the information given below, can you tell how many gemstones of each kind were taken?

1. There are more aquamarines than peridots.

2. There are fewer than 4 pieces of turquoise.

3. There are at least two more garnets than agates.

4. There are more peridots than garnets.

ANSWER ON PAGE 153.

OVERHEARD INFORMATION (PART 1)

Read the story below, then turn the page and answer the questions.

The detective overheard the thief tell her accomplice about the different places where she stashed the loot. She said, "I wanted to put the art forgery out in the open, but alas, too risky, so it's in a plastic bin underneath the bed. The diamonds are in the safe up in the attic. I've tucked the ruby necklace in the toe of some fuzzy slippers than I never wear. The bottle of wine is hiding in plain sight in the wine cellar with a fake label showing a bulldog."

OVERHEARD INFORMATION (PART II)

(Do not read this until you have read the previous page!)

1. The art forgery is found here.

   A. Attic safe

   B. Hung on the wall in the open

   C. Under the bed

   D. Wine cellar

2. What is found in the attic?

   A. Loose diamonds

   B. Diamond necklace

   C. Diamond bracelet

   D. Wine

3. The ruby necklace is tucked into these.

   A. Running shoes

   B. Fuzzy slippers

   C. Stiletto heels

   D. Pantyhose

4. The wine cellar has a fake label showing this kind of dog.

   A. Bulldog

   B. Boxer

   C. Terrier

   D. Unknown

ANSWERS ON PAGE 153.

MOTEL HIDEOUT

A thief hides out in one of the 45 motel rooms listed in the chart below. The motel's in-house detective received a sheet of four clues, signed "The Brilliant Thief." Using these clues, the detective found the room number within 15 minutes—but by that time, the thief had fled. Can you find the thief's motel room quicker?

1. The first digit is smaller than the second.

2. The second digit is not 3 or 4.

3. However, the number is divisible by 4.

4. The sum of the digits is more than 10.

51	52	53	54	55	56	57	58	59
41	42	43	44	45	46	47	48	49
31	32	33	34	35	36	37	38	39
21	22	23	24	25	26	27	28	29
11	12	13	14	15	16	17	18	19

ANSWER ON PAGE 153.

INTERCEPTION

You've intercepted a message that is meant to reveal a location for an upcoming meeting between two criminal masterminds. The only problem is, the message shows many place names. Can you figure out the right location?

CAIRO

SAN JOSE

NASSAU

LAREDO

MIAMI

ESWATINI

JAMAICA

ANSWER ON PAGE 153.

CRYPTO-LOGIC

Each of the numbers in the sequence below represents a letter. Use the mathematical clues to determine which number stands for which letter and reveal the encrypted word.

Hint: Remember that a / indicates divided by, and that all sums in parentheses must be done first.

36841285

$$A + L = B$$

$$L \times T = 12$$

$$T/2 = U$$

$$T - R = G$$

$$B + A = Y$$

$$T - M = Y$$

$$2B + U = T$$

$$L + M = 2G$$

$$L \times B = B$$

ANSWER ON PAGE 153.

UNSOLVED IN 1536

Every word listed is contained within the group of letters. Words can be found in a straight line horizontally, vertically, or diagonally. They may be read either forward or backward.

Robert Pakington, London merchant, was murdered by a handgun, perhaps the first person in London to be killed by that method.

AGNES (Spouse)

ANNE (Daughter)

ANTI-CLERICAL

CLOTH MERCHANT

"GRET REWARDE" (Offered)

ELIZABETH (Daughter)

HANDGUN

JOHN (Son)

KATHERINE (Spouse)

LONDON

MARGARET (Daughter)

MERCERS (Livery company)

MERCHANT

MURDER

PAKINGTON

NOVEMBER

PARLIAMENT (Member of)

PROTESTANT

ROBERT (Burial)

THOMAS (Son)

U J O L X N M E R C E R S J Q O
A T T K A A I I M O B J N K T H
G N O E H C N A J U E W A G N S
F A T U A K I O O S R T E Q E E
I H R Y N R H R V E H D S E M S
M C E R D N M O E E D S E A A Q
M R B V G B E X R L M G J R I L
E E O F U V R I I Z C B K H L O
R M R K N R N Y R T P I E T R N
C H S R D E W P Q G H L T R A D
H T E D R A W E R T E R G N P O
A O Y Q P R O T E S T A N T A N
N L S E N G A L Z W A N N E K L
T C Y S T E R A G R A M R Z H F
W M O B H T E B A Z I L E M Y Z
W P A K I N G T O N S A M O H T

FIND THE WITNESS

On Honeycrisp Street, there are 5 houses. You need to gather a witness statement from Javier Ceballos, but without any address on the doors you are not sure which house to approach. You know that Ceballos is a single man who lives by himself. The staff at the sandwich shop around the corner and your own observations give you some clues. From the information given, can you find the right house?

A. One member of the wait staff says Mr. Ceballos lives at one of the two blue houses on the street.

B. Another member of the wait staff knows that a family lives in house C.

C. House D is green.

D. The house at one end of the street is red; the house at the other end is white.

House A

House B

House C

House D

House E

ANSWER ON PAGE 154.

WHAT CHANGED? (PART I)

Study this picture for one minute, then turn the page.

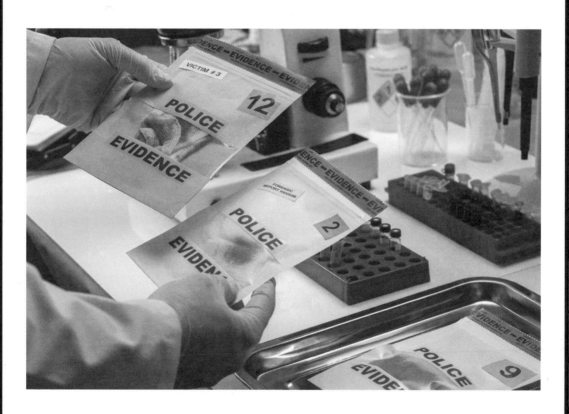

WHAT CHANGED? (PART II)

(Do not read this until you have read the previous page!)

From memory, can you tell what changed between this and the previous page?

ANSWER ON PAGE 154.

OVERHEARD INFORMATION (PART 1)

Read the story below, then turn the page and answer the questions.

The detective overheard the jewelry thief tell her accomplice about the different places where she stashed the loot. She said, "The diamond tiara is on the shelf of the spare room closet at the condo in New York City. I've tucked away the emeralds in the kitchen there, but I'm not going to say exactly where. The rubies are in the basement in the house in Los Angeles. The pearls are right out in the open in the house in Maine. I've got them in a vase with a bunch of colorful cheap beads."

OVERHEARD INFORMATION (PART II)

(Do not read this until you have read the previous page!)

1. The diamonds are found in this room.

    A. Main bedroom

    B. Spare bedroom

    C. Kitchen

    D. Living room

2. The rubies are found at that location.

    A. House in New York

    B. Condo in New York

    C. House in Los Angeles

    D. Condo in Los Angeles

3. What jewels are hidden in Maine?

    A. Diamonds

    B. Rubies

    C. Emeralds

    D. Pearls

4. The emeralds are found in this room.

    A. Main bedroom

    B. Spare bedroom

    C. Kitchen

    D. Living room

ANSWERS ON PAGE 154.

WHAT'S THE CRIME?

The following phrases are all anagrams for a specific crime. What is it?

CONCLUDED DRY RIOTS

OCCLUDED RIND STORY

SORRY CONDUCTED LID

CIRCLED DUSTY DONOR

ANSWER ON PAGE 154.

TRACK THE FUGITIVE

The investigator is tracking the fugitive's past trips in order to find and recover information that was left behind in five cities. Each city was visited only once. Can you put together the travel timeline, using the information below?

1. Raleigh and Tuscon were visited back-to-back, not necessarily in that order.

2. Wichita was not the third or fourth city visited.

3. From Saint Paul, the fugitive went to another city and then to Philadelphia.

4. The visits to Saint Paul and Raleigh were separated by visits to two other cities.

ANSWER ON PAGE 154.

FINGERPRINT MATCH

Find the matching fingerprint(s). There may be more than one.

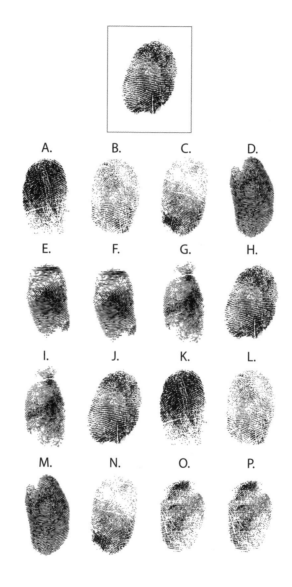

A.   B.   C.   D.

E.   F.   G.   H.

I.   J.   K.   L.

M.   N.   O.   P.

ANSWER(S) ON PAGE 154.

STOLEN GEMS

Unscramble each word or phrase below to reveal a gem that might be stolen.

MAID NOD

THY MEATS

ASIA ZIP LULL

ARCANE NIL

AIM CHALET

OUR AILMENT

MANQUE ARIA

CHANCY DOLE

ANSWERS ON PAGE 154.

SEEN AT THE SCENE (PART 1)

Study this picture for 1 minute, then turn the page.

SEEN AT THE SCENE (PART II)

(Do not read this until you have read the previous page!)

Which image exactly matches the picture from the previous page?

1.

2.

3.

4.

ANSWER ON PAGE 155.

PICK YOUR POISON

There are five bottles before you, but they've gotten jumbled up. Poison is found in one of them. If you arrange them from left to right, following the instructions given below, you will be able to know where the poison is found.

1. The red bottle is not next to the blue bottle.

2. The green bottle is not next to the yellow bottle.

3. The purple bottle is in the middle.

4. The red bottle is to the left of the bottle with the poison, but three other bottles separate them.

5. The blue bottle is to the right of the purple bottle, but not immediately.

6. The bottle with the poison is next to a bottle with a primary color.

ANSWER ON PAGE 155.

UNSOLVED IN 679

Every word listed is contained within the group of letters. Words can be found in a straight line horizontally, vertically, or diagonally. They may be read either forward or backward.

Dagobert II was a Frankish king in the Merovingian dynasty who ruled for a few short years until a selection of the nobility conspired to have him assassinated.

AUSTRASIA (Territory)

CIVIL WAR

CLOVIS (Predecessor)

DAGOBERT

EXILE (When his father died)

FRANKS

GOLD COINAGE (Reintroduced)

IRELAND (Place of exile)

LUCAFAO (Decisive battle)

MARSEILLE (Royal Mint)

MARTYR (Post-death)

MEROVINGIAN

**MONK
(During his time in Ireland)**

**NEUSTRIA
(Neighboring warring kingdom)**

SIGEBERT III (Father)

THEUDERIC III (Successor)

```
G H F A I S A R T S U A O Z L I
T H E B S A S D W F M D F I U C
J H A C E E C K D T V G I K C S
H M E E I K G H N U M I K M A H
S A G U F V H A A A T S F F F P
X R N A D C I S N R R M K C A X
L T A A O E K L E I A F D N O E
S Y I E I C R B W R O N F V C H
I R G E D R E I S A A C K E Y Y
V S N O X G T E C L R N D L C B
O H I F I I S E I O P K L W H
L Z V S E L L R U M I E O J O H
C M O H L L I E N E R I S N I G
V K R E P G M S U Z N G I I A J
E M E B G D A G O B E R T O E M
L D M H I X F Z P N I M N G R G
```

AN EARLY AMERICAN KIDNAPPING

Cryptograms are messages in substitution code. Break the code to read the message. For example, THE SMART CAT might become FVO QWGDF JGF if **F** is substituted for **T**, **V** for **H**, **O** for **E**, and so on.

XE 1874, FGPL-WKSL-GAM VTSLAKW LGNN SEM TXN

FXQK-WKSL-GAM ZLGOTKL RKLK HASWXEJ XE FLGEO GF OTKXL

HTXASMKAHTXS TGCK RTKE ORG CKE GFFKLXEJ VSEMW SEM

FXLKRGLDN SNDKM OTK ZLGOTKLN OG JG RXOT OTKC. RSAOKL

RSN MLGHHKM GFF SO S NOGLK, ZPO OTK CKE MXNSHHKSLXEJ

RXOT VTSLAKW XE OTKXL VSLLXSJK. OTK LGNN FSCXAW ZKJSE

LKVKXQXEJ LSENGC EGOKN, SEM OTK VSNK LKVKXQKM TKSQW

HLKNN VGQKLSJK. VTSLAKW LGNN RSN EKQKL NKKE SJSXE. ORG

VSLKKL VLXCXESAN RTG RKLK VSPJTO RTXAK LGZZXEJ S TGPNK

ASOKL OTSO WKSL RKLK ZKAXKQKM OG ZK OTK DXMESHHKLN.

OVERHEARD INFORMATION (PART I)

Read the story below, then turn the page and answer the questions.

An investigator hears a conversation between two criminals, in which one tells the other the passwords to the underground gambling clubs run through his chain of restaurants. She hears, "At the Purple Heron, tell the server, 'Is Rochelle working today? Can I go back to see her just for a moment?' At the Blue Pelican, talk to the host, not any of the servers, and ask if the grilled sea bass is on the menu tonight, because Georgie said good things about it. Only go to the Pink Pig on Thursdays and Fridays, and tell the server, 'I'd like the Pink Pig cocktail special, and can you make sure it's in a pink glass?'"

OVERHEARD INFORMATION (PART II)

(Do not read this until you have read the previous page!)

1. At which restaurant is the person told to ask for Rochelle?

  A. Purple Heron

  B. Blue Heron

  C. Blue Pelican

  D. Pink Pelican

2. At the Blue Pelican, the person is told to speak to:

  A. Any server

  B. The host

  C. Georgie

  D. The owner

3. The Pink Pig gambling club only runs on these days:

  A. Fridays and Saturdays

  B. Saturdays and Sundays

  C. Tuesdays and Thursdays

  D. Thursdays and Fridays

4. At one location, the person should ask about this dish on the menu.

  A. Pan fried sea bass

  B. Grilled sea bass

  C. Baked salmon

  D. Cedar-plank salmon

ANSWERS ON PAGE 155.

FIND THE WITNESS

On Stevens Avenue, there are 5 houses that are identical to each other. You need to follow up with a witness, Tamika Benjamin, but without any address on the doors you are not sure which house to approach. You know that Benjamin is a single mom and that her daughter Lorraine owns a dog. The staff at the ice cream shop around the corner and your own observations give you some clues. From the information given, can you find the right house?

A. Only two children live full-time on the street, and they live next door to each other.

B. The divorced man in house D has custody of his kids 3 weekends a month.

C. The people in both corner houses have cats, not dogs.

D. Lorraine used to come into the ice cream shop with her next door neighbor and babysitter Anselm, but Anselm is off at college now, and his parents are thinking of moving to a smaller place for "empty nesters."

House A   House B   House C   House D   House E

ANSWER ON PAGE 155.

CRYPTO-LOGIC

Each of the numbers in the sequence below represents a letter. Use the mathematical clues to determine which number stands for which letter and reveal the encrypted word.

Hint: Remember that a / indicates divided by, and that all sums in parentheses must be done first.

49252

R + 7 = P

2A = P

R X S = S

P - S = B

S cubed = L

I X A = P

I + B + 1 = P

ANSWER ON PAGE 156.

WHAT CHANGED? (PART I)

Study this picture for one minute, then turn the page.

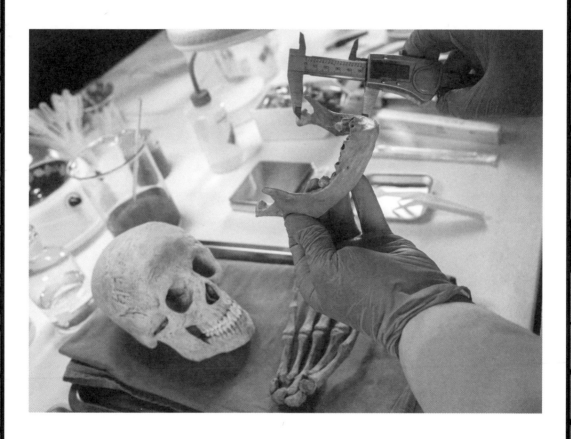

WHAT CHANGED? (PART II)

(Do not read this until you have read the previous page!)

From memory, can you tell what changed between this and the previous page?

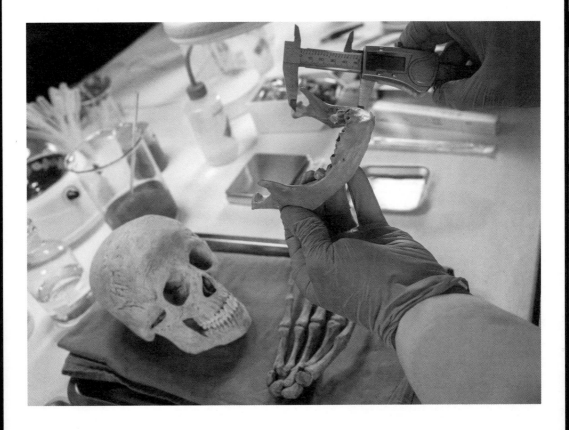

ANSWER ON PAGE 156.

WORD LADDER

Use the clues to change just one letter on each line to go from the top word to the bottom word. Do not change the order of the letters. You must have a common English word at each step.

VEIN

_____ lift it to kiss the bride

_____ meat of calves

_____ genuine

_____ ...what you sow"

_____ a common word for bound

_____ ...and they will follow

DEAD

MOTEL HIDEOUT

A thief hides out in one of the 45 motel rooms listed in the chart below. The motel's in-house detective received a sheet of four clues, signed "The Sober Thief." Using these clues, the detective found the room number within 15 minutes—but by that time, the thief had fled. Can you find the thief's motel room quicker?

1. Both digits are odd numbers.

2. The first digit is less than the second digit.

3. The sum of the digits is 8 or less.

4. It is divisible by 5 and 7.

51	52	53	54	55	56	57	58	59
41	42	43	44	45	46	47	48	49
31	32	33	34	35	36	37	38	39
21	22	23	24	25	26	27	28	29
11	12	13	14	15	16	17	18	19

ANSWER ON PAGE 156.

SPOT THE VEHICLE

Spot the car of the suspect in the parking lot.

ANSWER ON PAGE 156.

THE GEM THIEF

A company that sold gems found that 5 types of gems had been stolen from their warehouse. There was 1 gem of the first type, 2 of the second type, 3 of the third type, 4 of the fourth type, and 5 of the fifth type. From the information given below, can you tell how many gemstones of each kind were taken?

1. There are either 3 or 4 emeralds.

2. There are either 1 or 2 amethysts.

3. There are not 4 zircons.

4. There are more opals than emeralds.

5. There are either 4 or 5 garnets.

6. There are two more opals than amethysts.

ANSWER ON PAGE 156.

FIND THE WITNESS

There are 5 houses on Maple Lane. You need to gather a witness statement from Tajiya Khan, but without any address on the doors you are not sure which house to approach. You know that Khan is a single woman who lives by herself. The staff at the cafe around the corner and your own observations give you some clues. From the information given, can you find the right house?

A. One member of the waitstaff says Khan lives at one of the two blue houses on the street.

B. Another waiter knows that a family lives in house D.

C. House B is yellow.

D. The corner houses are white.

House A   House B   House C   House D   House E

ANSWER ON PAGE 156.

BAT MASTERSON

Every word listed is contained within the group of letters. Words can be found in a straight line horizontally, vertically, or diagonally. They may be read either forward or backward.

ARMY SCOUT

BARTHOLOMEW

BAT

BOXING

BUFFALO HUNTER

DODGE CITY

DODGE CITY WAR

FRONTIER

GAMBLER

GREAT PLAINS

GUNFIGHT

GUNSLINGER

JOURNALIST

KANSAS

LAWMAN

MASTERSON

PRIZEFIGHTING

QUEBEC (Birthplace)

SHERIFF

SPORTSWRITER

THEODORE ROOSEVELT (Friend)

WILD WEST

```
T S I L A N R U O J T S E H X B A W
Z G N I X O B H K V H M U L S C O E
U M F K M D A R A R E L B M A G Q M
O X G B A T B A N T O L Q C P U D O
L A R N F T G W S P D N H R E O V L
G F E O J S V Y A R O X I B A R T O
Z O A S P E M T S D R Z E X N E U H
N D T R S W A I M E E C G Q A T O T
B O P E E D H C D F R J U G M N C R
D D L T I L O E I F O I N U W U S A
F G A S P I J G Y F O R F N A H Y B
R E I A S W H D C I S Q I S L O M S
O C N M Q T Z O Q R E I G L E L R Y
N I S L I O H D W E V G H I H A A Y
T T W N K V F H D H E P T N T F M F
I Y G C S E B O O S L L A G O F R N
E P A D C Y B N J P T D I E P U S M
R E T I R W S T R O P S O R I B I T
```

TRACK THE FUGITIVE

The investigator is tracking the fugitive's past trips in order to find and recover information that was left behind in five cities. Each city was visited only once. Can you put together the travel timeline, using the information below?

1. Boston is visited before Tulsa, but not immediately before.

2. From Juneau, the fugitive went right to a state on the Pacific coastline.

3. The fugitive did not visit New Orleans first or second.

4. San Jose was visited sometime before Boston.

ANSWER ON PAGE 157.

SEEN AT THE SCENE (PART I)

Study this picture for 1 minute, then turn the page.

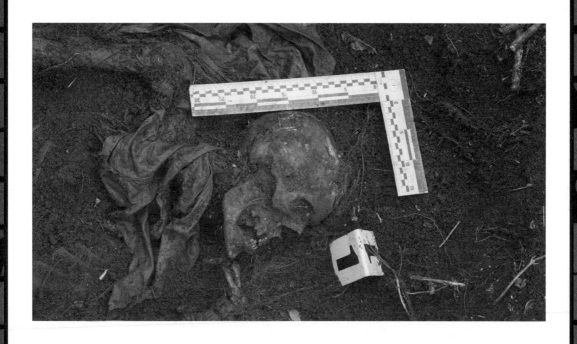

SEEN AT THE SCENE (PART II)

(Do not read this until you have read the previous page!)

Which image exactly matches the picture from the previous page?

1.
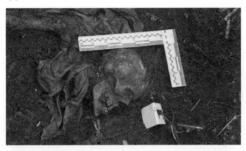

2.

3.

4.

ANSWER ON PAGE 157.

INTERCEPTION

You've intercepted a message that is meant to reveal a location for an upcoming meeting between two criminal masterminds. The only problem is, the message shows many place names. Can you figure out the right location?

HONOLULU

LONDON

LOUISVILLE

BOTSWANA

CROATIA

ECUADOR

CHATTANOOGA

ANSWER ON PAGE 157.

TIGER KING

Every word listed is contained within the group of letters. Words can be found in a straight line horizontally, vertically, or diagonally. They may be read either forward or backward.

ANIMALS	JOSHUA
BIG CATS	MINISERIES
BREEDING	NETFLIX
CAMPAIGN	PARK
CAROLE BASKIN	PLOT
CUBS	RESCUE
DILLON	RICK
DOC ANTLE	SANCTUARY
ECCENTRIC	SPECIES
ENDANGERED	TIGER KING
FEUD	TRAVIS
G.W. ZOO	TRUE CRIME
HUSBANDS	WILDLIFE
JOE EXOTIC	ZOOKEEPER
JOHN	

X N W U R E S C U E D U E F E
J M I N I S E R I E S Y J X S
O D L K C U B S N K E H O A I
S O D T S B P D P R M Y H U V
H C L O T A A J D A I R N H A
U A I L I N B O I P R A G S R
S N F P G I R E L Z C U I O T
B T E E E M E E L O E T A J P
A L R O R A E X O O U C P S N
N E R O K L D O N K R N M E E
D F I Z I S I T S E T A A I T
S Y C W N S N I P E R S C C F
P I K G G F G C E P E O G E L
R C I R T N E C C E S L I P I
B I G C A T S U I R C P B S X

ANSWERS ON PAGE 157.

FIND THE WITNESS

There are 5 houses on Mallard Avenue. You need to follow up with a witness, Roger Singleton, but the paperwork only lists his street, not his specific address. You know from the previous interview that Singleton lives with his girlfriend, and Singleton drives a motorcycle. The staff at the corner taproom and your own observations give you some clues. From the information given, can you find the right house?

A. Couples live in houses A, C, and D.

B. The brewmaster at the taproom knows Singleton lives next to a widow, because she used to complain about the noise of Singleton's motorcycle, but now she appreciates that Singleton rakes her leaves each November.

C. The bartender doesn't know which house the widow lives in, but she adds that the widow doesn't think as highly of the neighbor who lives on the other side of her.

D. Singleton's girlfriend was visiting the couple next door on the day he witnessed the crime.

House A   House B   House C   House D   House E

ANSWER ON PAGE 157.

DNA SEQUENCE

Examine the two images below carefully. Are these sequences a match or not?

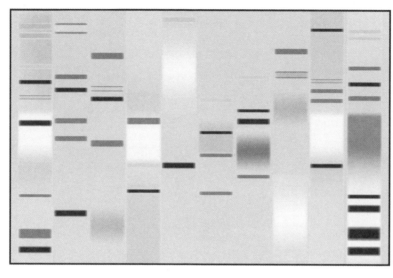

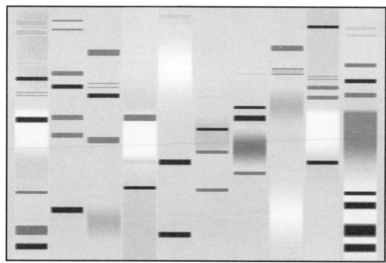

CASE NOT CLOSED

Every word listed is contained within the group of letters. Words can be found in a straight line horizontally, vertically, or diagonally. They may be read either forward or backward.

BIGGIE SMALLS	NATALIE WOOD
(The) BLACK DAHLIA	NICOLE BROWN
D.B. COOPER	ROANOKE
DIAN FOSSEY	RON GOLDMAN
EDGAR ALLEN POE	SEVERED FEET MYSTERY
GARDNER MUSEUM	TUPAC SHAKUR
JACK THE RIPPER	TYLENOL POISONINGS
JIMMY HOFFA	(The) WATCHER
MARILYN SHEPPARD	(The) ZODIAC KILLINGS

```
R B E L O C I N N O S I O P L O N E L Y T
P I R E H T K C A J J N A M D L O G N O R
S S O F N A I D I N A T A L I E W O O D E
Y T V B G M Z P O G C B D Y H O H J A S P
J U Z M A S O T K O K B T O K O R F H Z O
S E V E R E D F E E T M Y S T E R Y S K O
S D P L D I I A R L H A L R R V B B C N C
Y G P D N G A B H T E R E N C P Z L A W B
M A E I E G C L O H R I N M B S I C P O D
T R H A R I K A O A I L O D J P B B U R Z
E A S N M B I C T D P Y L L K I N F T B O
E L N F U T L K U K P N P O G S E R J E D
F L Y O S R L D P C E S O G N U L O I L I
D E L S E E I A A A R H I N A M L A M O A
E N B S U H N H C L J E S A T R A N M C C
R P R E M C G L S B S P O R A E R O Y I K
E O A Y A T S I H M H P N M L N A K H N I
V E M N L A C A A G C A I V I D G E O G L
E D G P B W F L K I T R N P E R D U F O L
S O N A O R L S U J A D G P W A E P F W I
Z N J U T S O D R Y W S S D Z G I A A W M
```

MOTEL HIDEOUT

A thief hides out in one of the 45 motel rooms listed in the chart below. The motel's in-house detective received a sheet of four clues, signed "The Logical Thief." Using these clues, the detective found the room number—but by that time, the thief had fled. Can you find the thief's motel room more quickly?

1. The sum of the digits is greater than 10.

2. The number is not a multiple of 7.

3. The number is not prime.

4. The number is a multiple of 4.

51	52	53	54	55	56	57	58	59
41	42	43	44	45	46	47	48	49
31	32	33	34	35	36	37	38	39
21	22	23	24	25	26	27	28	29
11	12	13	14	15	16	17	18	19

ANSWER ON PAGE 158.

WHAT CHANGED? (PART I)

Study this picture for one minute, then turn the page.

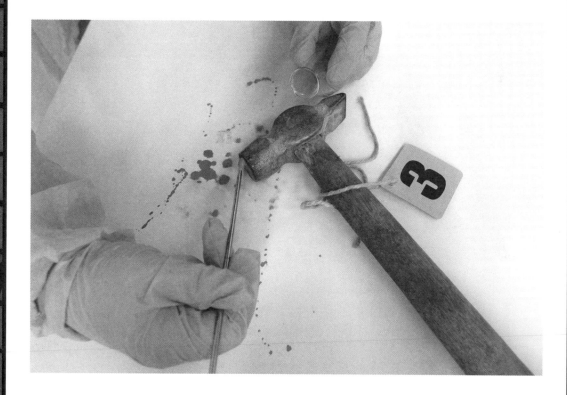

WHAT CHANGED? (PART II)

(Do not read this until you have read the previous page!)

From memory, can you tell what changed between this and the previous page?

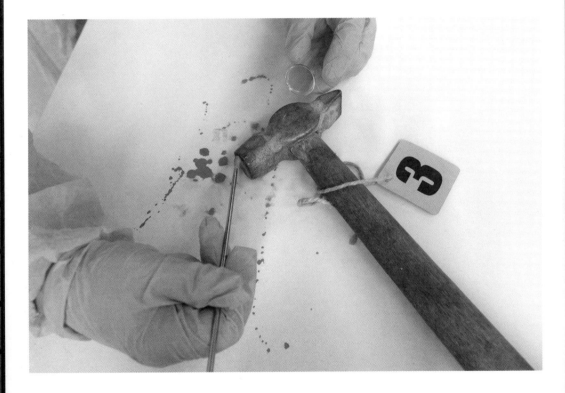

ANSWER ON PAGE 158.

OVERHEARD INFORMATION (PART I)

Read the story below, then turn the page and answer the questions.

The detective overheard the jewelry thief tell his accomplice about the different places where he stashed the loot. He said, "The gold bars are in a shoe box underneath a stack of magazines in the walk-in closet. The emeralds are taped in a sealed bag underneath the sink in the second floor bathroom. The opal bracelet is with my girl, but she's promised not to wear it in public for three years. The rubies are tucked into the corner of the frame of the vintage auto poster in the den."

OVERHEARD INFORMATION (PART II)

(Do not read this until you have read the previous page!)

1. The gold bars are found in this location.

       A. Hall closet

       B. Walk-in closet

       C. Bathroom

       D. Dining room

2. The emeralds are found in a bathroom on this level.

       A. Basement

       B. First floor

       C. Second floor

       D. Attic

3. The thief's girlfriends has promised not to wear this/these for three years.

       A. Opal bracelet

       B. Opal necklace

       C. Opal earrings

       D. Ruby tiara

4. The rubies are found in the frame of this artwork.

       A. Landscape painting

       B. Landscape poster

       C. Vintage auto poster

       D. The subject of the artwork is not specified.

ANSWERS ON PAGE 158.

WHAT CHANGED? (PART I)

Study this picture for one minute, then turn the page.

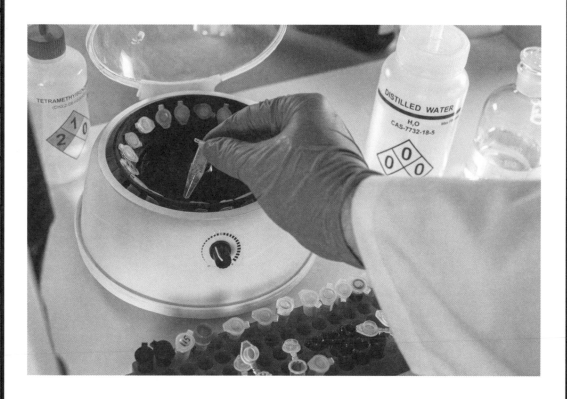

WHAT CHANGED? (PART II)

(Do not read this until you have read the previous page!)

From memory, can you tell what changed between this and the previous page?

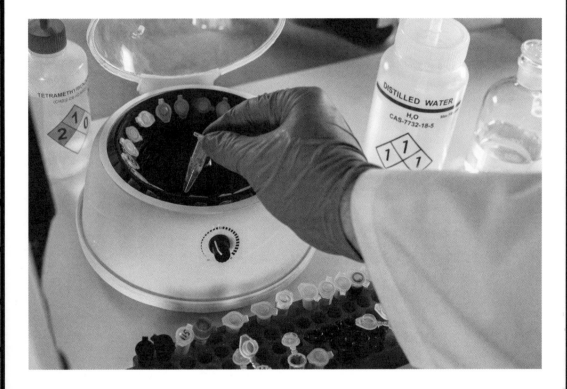

ANSWER ON PAGE 158.

FIND THE WITNESS

On Wilson Street, there are 5 houses that are identical to each other. You need to gather a witness statement from Jada Brown, but without any address on the doors you are not sure which house to approach. You know that Brown lives with her boyfriend and her teenaged son. The staff at the ice cream shop around the corner and your own observations give you some clues. From the information given, can you find the right house?

    A. The people who live in house B always help the elderly couple next door, whose children live far away, shovel their walkway.

    B. The elderly couple also get help from Jamil and Lee, who live on the other side of the elderly couple, and drive them to the grocery store each week.

    C. The couple in one corner house are excited about helping plan the upcoming wedding of their daughter.

    D. One house is vacant while it's being sold.

House A   House B   House C   House D   House E

ANSWER ON PAGE 159.

GREAT GUMSHOES

ACROSS

1. "Yesterday" or "Tomorrow"
5. Auction ender
9. Botanical balm
10. Boo-boo, to a tot
11. Rex Stout's detective
13. U.S. mil. award
14. Romance novelist Georgette
15. Home improvement letters
16. "Back in the Saddle ___"
19. A dance, when doubled
22. "The Bungalow Mystery" solver
24. Fork part
25. Chophouse order
26. Slaughter in baseball
27. Barnyard mothers

DOWN

1. Beach, basically
2. Barcelona bravos
3. "Cheers" regular
4. Prefix that means "earth"
5. Cry on a hog farm
6. Comic-book wise bird
7. Board game or cereal
8. Animal at a salt lick
12. Complaining a lot
15. Cuts into cubes
16. Chip into a pot
17. Football yardage
18. ___ domini
19. Stick in one's ___ (rankle)
20. Roll call reply
21. Knocks out, in a way
23. Dr. of rap

1	2	3	4	█	5	6	7	8
9				█	10			
11				12				
13			█	14				
█	█	█	15			█	█	█
16	17	18			█	19	20	21
22					23			
24				█	25			
26				█	27			

MOTEL HIDEOUT

A thief hides out in one of the 45 motel rooms listed in the chart below. The motel's in-house detective received a sheet of four clues, signed "The Logical Thief." Using these clues, the detective found the room number—but by that time, the thief had fled. Can you find the thief's motel room more quickly?

1. The number is not a multiple of 5.

2. The digit 1 is not found in the number.

3. The number is either a square or a cube number.

4. The sum of the digits is not 9.

51	52	53	54	55	56	57	58	59
41	42	43	44	45	46	47	48	49
31	32	33	34	35	36	37	38	39
21	22	23	24	25	26	27	28	29
11	12	13	14	15	16	17	18	19

ANSWER ON PAGE 159.

SEEN AT THE SCENE (PART I)

Study this picture for one minute, then turn the page.

SEEN AT THE SCENE (PART II)

(Do not read this until you have read the previous page!)

Which image exactly matches the picture from the previous page?

1.

2.

3.

4.

ANSWER ON PAGE 159.

FIND THE WITNESS

On Loomis Court, there are 5 houses that are identical to each other. You need to follow up with a witness, Betty Perkins, but without any address on the doors you are not sure which house to approach. You know that from a previous statement that Perkins and her husband have two children, both girls. The staff at the corner coffee shop and your own observations give you some clues. From the information given, can you find the right house?

A. One staff member says she knows that the couple in house B do not have children, but every other house has at least one child living in it.

B. Another staff member isn't sure where Perkins lives, but he says he's heard her say that she's lucky that her next door neighbor has a girl the same age as hers.

C. The retired couple who have custody of their grandson do not live in a corner house.

D. Both kids who live in the corner houses are only children.

House A   House B   House C   House D   House E

ANSWER ON PAGE 159.

TRACK THE FUGITIVE

The investigator is tracking the fugitive's past trips in order to find and recover information that was left behind in five cities. Each city was visited only once. Can you put together the travel timeline, using the information below?

1. The two cities in Kentucky were not visited consecutively.

2. Lexington was visited sometime after Jersey City.

3. Louisville was visited sometime before Miami.

4. Atlanta was not visited third.

5. The fugitive went to the city in Florida, then two other cities, then the city in Georgia.

ANSWER ON PAGE 159.

THE GEM THIEF

A company that sold gems found that 5 types of gems had been stolen from their warehouse. There was 1 gem of the first type, 2 of the second type, 3 of the third type, 4 of the fourth type, and 5 of the fifth type. From the information given below, can you tell how many gemstones of each kind were taken?

1. There are not 4 diamonds.

2. There are two more amethysts than opals.

3. There are either 3 or 5 pieces of topaz.

4. There are fewer amethysts than pieces of jade.

5. Diamonds are not the least plentiful gem.

ANSWER ON PAGE 160.

BASS REEVES

Every word listed is contained within the group of letters. Words can be found in a straight line horizontally, vertically, or diagonally. They may be read either forward or backward.

APPREHENSION

ARKANSAS

ARRESTS

BASS

BORN IN SLAVERY

CRIMINALS

DEPUTY U.S. MARSHAL

ESCAPED

FARMER

FREEDMAN

LAW ENFORCEMENT

MARKSMAN

MULTILINGUAL

MUSKOGEE

NO SERIOUS INJURIES

OKLAHOMA TERRITORY

REEVES

WEST

```
J  O  D  L  P  A  R  K  A  N  S  A  S  A  O  D  S  L
A  L  K  E  A  H  H  G  F  V  S  F  I  C  T  E  S  A
P  N  A  L  P  U  C  B  I  D  R  T  A  N  I  E  J  W
P  A  E  H  A  A  G  G  L  S  Z  C  S  R  V  V  J  E
R  M  I  V  S  H  C  N  L  U  Y  S  U  E  M  Q  T  N
E  D  B  W  L  R  O  S  I  J  B  J  E  L  R  E  G  F
H  E  U  O  B  F  A  M  E  L  N  R  U  I  Q  R  R  O
E  E  T  L  R  N  C  M  A  I  I  T  B  G  S  X  A  R
N  R  E  S  Y  N  G  R  S  T  E  T  U  A  S  E  H  C
S  F  H  B  E  X  I  U  I  U  E  M  L  G  A  M  N  E
I  E  R  C  N  W  O  N  D  M  Y  R  H  U  B  F  A  M
O  M  E  S  V  I  I  B  S  B  I  T  R  U  M  R  F  E
N  L  J  G  R  M  R  E  I  L  E  N  U  I  U  A  A  N
Y  K  B  E  O  A  J  Q  W  C  A  Y  A  P  T  T  J  T
X  B  S  N  J  K  G  V  Q  K  E  V  R  L  E  O  V  V
X  O  B  Z  T  U  S  X  L  D  E  J  E  E  S  D  R  R
N  E  U  P  X  H  C  U  A  Z  I  A  U  R  I  E  E  Y
N  A  M  S  K  R  A  M  M  Y  U  A  C  V  Y  V  Z  W
```

ANSWERS ON PAGE 160.

ANSWERS

Super Sleuths
(pages 4-5)

¹A	²F	³R	⁴A	⁵I	⁶D		⁷L	T	⁸S
¹⁰R	O	O	T	O	N		¹¹A	I	T
¹²N	I	C	K	C	¹³A	R	T	E	R
¹⁴E	E	K	A		¹⁵L	O	T	T	A
			¹⁶G	A	P	E	A	T	
¹⁷H	¹⁸A	¹⁹R	²⁰R	Y	B	O	S	C	H
²¹A	D	E	E	M	S				
²²G	L	E	N	S		²³E	²⁴A	²⁵S	²⁶T
²⁷M	I	K	E	H	²⁸A	M	M	E	R
²⁹A	B	O		³⁰O	R	I	O	L	E
³¹N	S	F		³²E	E	R	I	L	Y

A Murderer in the House
(page 6)

What I feel is that if one has got to have a murder actually happening in one's house, one might as well enjoy it, if you know what I mean. — Agatha Christie, "The Body in the Library"

Bank Mayhem
(page 7)

The answer is 64.

The Gem Thief
(page 8)

The count is: 1 sapphire, 2 agates, 3 pearls, 4 turquoises, 5 rubies, and 6 diamonds.

Sniffing Out the Evidence
(page 9)

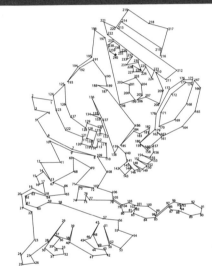

ANSWERS

Unsolved in Australia
(pages 10-11)

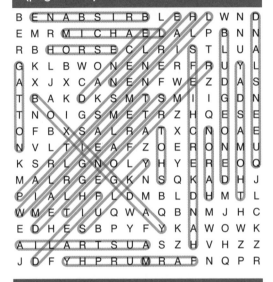

DNA Sequence
(page 15)

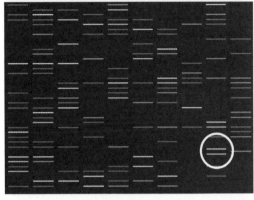

Fingerprint Match
(page 12)

G is the matching fingerprint.

What Changed?
(pages 13-14)

A plant disappeared.

Interception
(page 16)

Take the central letter of each word, reading upward, to reveal: town square

A Horrific Home Invasion
(pages 17-18)

1. A. Hinterkaifeck; 2. False; 3. C. 1922; 4. B. A mattock

ANSWERS

Hostilities of Television
(page 19)

Seeing a murder on television can help work off one's antagonisms. And if you haven't any antagonisms, the commercials will give you some.
— Alfred Hitchcock

Badge Carrying
(pages 20-21)

S	G	T		P	E	P		I	F	N	O	T
T	A	J		E	P	A		G	R	O	V	E
U	S	H	E	R	I	N		N	A	V	E	L
	P	O	L	I	C	E	W	O	M	A	N	
	O	I	L	S		H	R	E				
T	Y	K	E	S		C	O	E	R	C	E	S
A	D	E			G	S	A			O	W	E
I	S	R	A	E	L	I		M	E	L	E	E
			D	D	E		A	U	L	D		
	S	A	V	I	N	G	G	R	A	C	E	
M	I	D	I	S		A	I	R	M	A	I	L
A	N	D	S	O		G	L	O		S	R	O
E	S	S	E	N		S	E	W		E	E	G

Person of Interest
(page 22)

Seen at the Scene
(pages 23-24)

Picture 2 is a match.

ANSWERS

A Crime Boss Topples
(pages 25-26)

1. C. 1902–1920; 2. B. Victoria Moresco; 3. False; 4. Restaurant

Treasure Hunt
(page 27)

The order is: rubies, sapphires, pearls, gold coins, silver necklace, bronze tiara.

Unsolved in 1876
(pages 28-29)

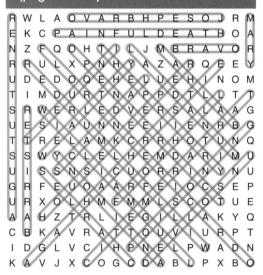

Fingerprint Match
(page 30)

G and I are the matching fingerprints.

Interception
(page 31)

Take the first letter of the second word in each place name to reveal: California

Crypto-logic
(page 32)

HOMICIDE

DNA Sequence
(page 33)

They are a match.

Most Boastful
(page 34)

I do have a sneaking admiration for anyone who has the intelligence to plan a job properly and the courage to carry it out. As long as no one gets hurt and the target is a bank or an insurance company. — Karl Wiggins

ANSWERS

What Changed?
(pages 35-36)

The bullet casings changed places.

Jail Cell
(page 37)

JAIL, bail, ball, bell, CELL

Bail Bond
(page 37)

Answers may vary. Four step: BAIL, ball, bald, band, BOND. Five steps: BAIL, sail, said, sand, band, BOND

Women of Mystery
(pages 38-39)

ANSWERS

Person of Interest
(page 40)

Murder at Lava Lake
(pages 41-42)

1. Deschutes National Forest; 2. Bend;
3. Roy Wilson; Dewey Morris; 4. Lee
Collins

Fingerprint Match
(page 43)

J is the matching fingerprint.

Unsolved in 1841
(pages 44-45)

Motel Hideout
(page 46)

The thief is in room 25.

Interception
(page 47)

Take the first letter of each word to
reveal: Eiffel Tower

Crypto-logic
(page 48)

DRUGS

ANSWERS

DNA Sequence
(page 49)

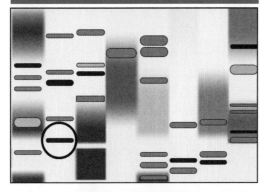

The Gem Thief
(page 50)

The count is: 1 turquoise, 2 emeralds, 3 pieces of topaz, 4 rubies, and 5 diamonds.

Seen at the Scene
(pages 51-52)

Picture 1 is a match.

Track the Fugitive
(page 53)

The order is: Memphis, El Paso, Fresno, Baltimore, San Antonio

Something Is Afoot
(pages 54-55)

Person of Interest
(page 56)

ANSWERS

Priest, Gangster, Politician
(pages 57-58)

1. 1872; 2. Counterfeiting; 3. Nineteenth;
4. John Powers

An Unsolved Crash
(page 59)

In 1923, a young, daring aviator died at the age of 31. B.H. DeLay owned an airfield, performed barnstorming stunts, and did stunt aviation in the movies. He also trained other pilots in stunt aviation for Hollywood. In 1923, he was doing a show when his plane plummeted to the ground in the middle of a loop-de-loop, killing him and his passenger. It was soon found to be no simple crash. Pins in the plane's wings were found to be of substandard size, pointing to sabotage. No one was ever charged with the crime.

Unsolved in 1682
(pages 60-61)

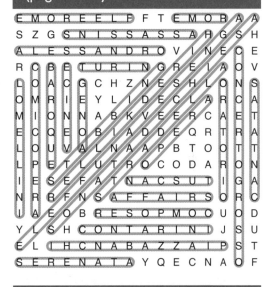

Fingerprint Match
(page 62)

F, G, and L are the matching fingerprints.

Overheard Information
(page 63-64)

1. A; 2. B; 3. D; 4. D

ANSWERS

Motel Hideout
(page 65)

The answer is 42.

Interception
(page 66)

Take the first and last letter of each place name to reveal: Main Street

What Changed?
(pages 67-68)

An additional leaf blew into frame.

Pick Your Poison
(page 69)

From left to right, the bottles are yellow, purple, green, blue, red. The poison is in the purple bottle.

Crypto-logic
(page 70)

MURDER

Find the Witness
(page 71)

Wright lives in house D.

Unsolved in 1678
(pages 72-73)

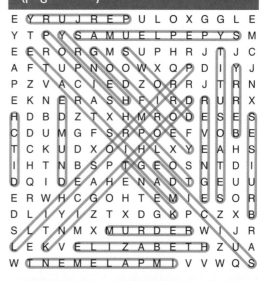

DNA Sequence
(page 74)

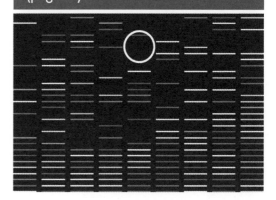

ANSWERS

Seen at the Scene
(pages 75-76)

Picture 2 is a match.

The Green Bicycle Case
(pages 77-78)

1. B. Factory worker; B. Joseph Cowell; 3. C. George Measures; 4. C. February 1920

Unsolved in New Jersey
(page 79)

In 1922, the bodies of a man and a woman were found in a field. They had both been shot. A hat covered the man's face, and his calling card was found at his feet. The man, Edward Hall, was an Episcopalian priest married to Frances Hall. The woman, Eleanor Mills, married to James Mills, was a member of the church choir. The two had been having an affair, and their love letters were left between their bodies. While Frances and her brothers were accused and tried for the crime in 1926, they were acquitted for lack of evidence and because witnesses claimed that one brother had been fishing with them.

The Gem Thief
(page 80)

The count is: 1 agate, 2 pieces of turquoise, 3 garnets, 4 peridots, and 5 aquamarines.

Overheard Information
(pages 81-82)

1. C; 2. A; 3. B; 4. A

Motel Hideout
(page 83)

The thief is in room 56.

Interception
(page 84)

Take the last two letters of each place name to reveal: Roseau, Dominica

Crypto-logic
(page 85)

BURGLARY

ANSWERS

Unsolved in 1536
(pages 86-87)

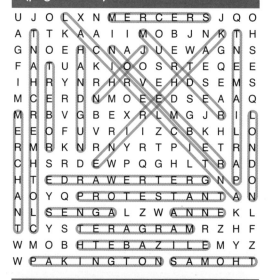

Find the Witness
(page 88)

Ceballos is in house B.

What Changed?
(pages 89-90)

On the evidence bag, the number 12 became a 2.

Overheard Information
(pages 91-92)

1. B; 2. C; 3. D; 4. C

What's the Crime?
(page 93)

Disorderly conduct

Track the Fugitive
(page 94)

The order is: Saint Paul, Wichita, Philadelphia, Raleigh, Tucson

Fingerprint Match
(page 95)

H and J are the matching fingerprints.

Stolen Gems
(page 96)

Diamond; amethyst; lapis lazuli; carnelian; malachite; tourmaline; aquamarine; chalcedony

ANSWERS

Seen at the Scene
(pages 97-98)

Picture 1 is a match.

Pick Your Poison
(page 99)

From left to right, the bottles are red, green, purple, yellow, blue. The poison is found in the blue bottle.

Unsolved in 679
(pages 100-101)

```
G H F A I S A R T S U A O Z L I
T H E B S A S D W F M D F I U C
J H A C E E C K D T V G I K C S
H M E E I K G H N U M I K M A H
S A G U F V H A A A T S F F F P
X R N A D C I S N R R M K C A X
L T A A O E K L E I A F D N O E
S Y I E I C R B W R O N F V C H
I R G E D R E I S A A C K E Y Y
V S N O X G T E C L R N D L C B
O H I F I I I S E I O P K L W H
L Z V S E L L R U M I E O J O H
C M O H L L I E N E R I S N I G
V K R E P G M S U Z N G I I A J
E M E B G D A G O B E R T O E M
L D M H I X F Z P N I M N G R G
```

An Early American Kidnapping
(page 102)

In 1874, four-year-old Charley Ross and his five-year-old brother were playing in front of their Philadelphia home when two men offering candy and fireworks asked the brothers to go with them. Walter was dropped off at a store, but the men disappearing with Charley in their carriage. The Ross family began receiving ransom notes, and the case received heavy press coverage. Charley Ross was never seen again. Two career criminals who were caught while robbing a house later that year were believed to be the kidnappers.

Overheard Information
(pages 103-104)

1. A; 2. B; 3. D; 4. B

Find the Witness
(page 105)

The Benjamins live in house B.

ANSWERS

Crypto-logic
(page 106)

ALIBI

What Changed?
(pages 107-108)

The instrument in the metal tray disappeared.

Word Ladder
(page 109)

VEIN, veil, veal, real, reap, leap, lead, DEAD

Motel Hideout
(page 110)

The thief is in room 35.

Spot the Vehicle
(page 111)

The Gem Thief
(page 112)

The count is: 1 zircon, 2 amethysts, 3 emeralds, 4 opals, and 5 garnets.

Find the Witness
(page 113)

Khan lives in house C.

ANSWERS

Bat Masterson
(pages 114-115)

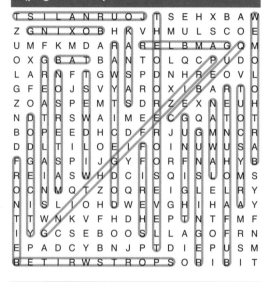

Track the Fugitive
(page 116)

The order is: Juneau, San Jose, Boston, New Orleans, Tulsa

Seen at the Scene
(pages 117-118)

Picture 2 is a match.

Interception
(page 119)

Take the first letter of the first word, the second letter of the second word, the third letter of the third word, the fourth letter of the fourth word, and so forth until you reveal that the criminal is hidden in Houston.

Tiger King
(pages 120-121)

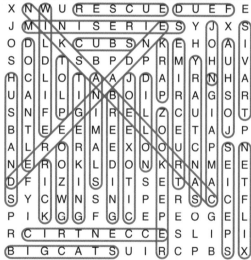

Find the Witness
(page 122)

Singleton lives in house C.

ANSWERS

DNA Sequence
(page 123)

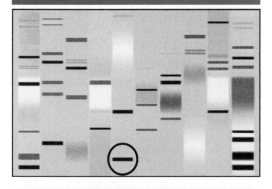

Case Not Closed
(pages 124-125)

Motel Hideout
(page 126)

The answer is 48.

What Changed?
(pages 127-128)

Part of the thread around the hammer disappeared.

Overheard Information
(pages 129-130)

1. B; 2. C; 3. A; 4. C

What Changed?
(pages 131-132)

The numbers on the bottle to the right changed.

ANSWERS

Find the Witness
(page 133)

Brown lives in house B.

Great Gumshoes
(pages 134-135)

Motel Hideout
(page 136)

The answer is 49.

Seen at the Scene
(pages 137-138)

Picture 4 is a match.

Find the Witness
(page 139)

Perkins lives in house D.

Track the Fugitive
(page 140)

The order is: Louisville, Miami, Jersey City, Lexington, Atlanta

ANSWERS

The Gem Thief
(page 141)

The count is: 1 opal, 2 diamonds, 3 amethysts, 4 pieces of jade, and 5 pieces of topaz.

Bass Reeves
(pages 142-143)

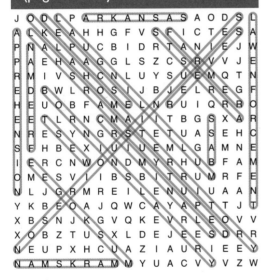